EVERYDAY MILLIONAIRES

How Ordinary People Built Extraordinary
Wealth—and How You Can Too

Command them to do good, to be rich in good deeds,
and to be generous and willing to share.

1 TIMOTHY 6:18

EVERYDAY MILLIONAIRES

*How Ordinary People Built Extraordinary
Wealth—and How You Can Too*

CHRIS HOGAN

RAMSEY
PRESS

Published by Ramsey Press, The Lampo Group, LLC
Brentwood, Tennessee 37027

Editors: Jen Gingerich and Allen Harris
Cover Design: Brad Dennison and Chris Carrico
Interior Design: Mandi Cofer

ISBN: 978-0-977489-52-7

Printed in the United States of America
19 20 21 22 23 RRD 5 4 3 2 1

Dedication

This book is dedicated to everyone who has dared to battle against challenges and overcome obstacles.

For the courageous people who have been doubted by others but who refused to allow others' opinions to become their limitations.

Your dreams are possible and worth the sacrifice and push it takes to achieve them.

Don't stop. You can do this! I believe in you!

And finally, to the Hogan boys—Tyson, Brock, and Case! Always remember that your daddy loves you so very much! You can achieve anything you put your mind, heart, and effort into! Dream big and work hard!

Acknowledgments

There is no way I would have been able to write *Everyday Millionaires* without the fantastic team of people I get to work with every day. I am forever grateful to:

Dave Ramsey, my mentor and friend. Thank you for your support, encouragement, and trust! You have spent your life chopping down myths so people could live their dreams!

Allen Harris, my editor. Thank you for helping me put the stories and research onto the page. You have incredible literary talents, my friend!

Jen Gingerich, my book guru! Thank you for leading this project from beginning to end. This book could not have happened without your input, guidance, and constant attention!

Preston Cannon, for helping shape and launch this project. You have been instrumental to every phase of this book. You are the book master!

Cody Bennett, for helping shape and guide the millionaire message and giving it your devoted time and attention. Your passion for the work we do inspires and energizes others.

Michelle Grooms, Rick Prall, and Pam Gibbs. Thank you for your incredible developmental and editorial support.

Luke LeFevre, Brad Dennison, and Chris Carrico, for having such creative vision for the design and cover.

Elizabeth Cole and McKenzie Masters, my publicity dream team. Thank you all for helping me share and spread this message across the nation!

Amy Warren, Tim Smith, and the Ramsey research team, for your diligence, effort, and pursuit of the incredible statistics and stories featured in this book!

Jeremy Breland, Suzanne Simms, Dawn Medley, Jen Sievertsen, Brian Williams, and the rest of our Ramsey Solutions team, for all of your time, effort, and energy spent in helping this idea become a reality. I am honored to work daily with each and every one of you!

Contents

CONTENTS

Foreword

Dave Ramsey

Have you ever done something you *thought* would work, but then it blew you away by exactly *how well* it worked? I'm talking about something that made such a huge impact that you were simultaneously shocked and proven right. I have. In 1994, I started teaching a little local money class called *Financial Peace University* (FPU). It was a labor of love for me. I had recently experienced a massive financial crash and getting out of that mess led me to a whole new way of handling money—an approach rooted in common sense, down-home wisdom, and biblical principles. I taught people the basics, things like saving, budgeting, and getting out of debt. But I also taught them how to invest and start planning for a radically different future. More than five million people have been through that class in the past twenty-five years, and, looking back on what we've seen from those families, I feel both vindicated and frustrated.

I feel vindicated because, as it turns out, God's ways of managing money actually work. People who went through the class and learned the principles from our books and radio show got out of debt. They got their lives under control. They started investing into their 401(k) and other retirement plans. They paid off their homes. And—*surprise*—they built wealth. As we continued to talk to and work with these people, we discovered they hadn't just gotten out of debt, but they had become millionaires! They had experienced a complete transformation in their finances, and they changed the entire trajectory of their families' lives. This stuff works!

However, I also felt frustrated. People were surprised that these millionaires started popping up. Even though we had talked about it for a quarter century, it was as though no one had ever heard us mention the likelihood of building wealth with these principles. People seemed to narrowly define me, our classes, our radio shows, and our books as the "get out of debt" material. Sure, that's always been a big part of our mission, but it was never the end goal. We didn't want people to get out of debt for the sake of getting out of debt; we wanted them to get out of debt *so that* they could build wealth . . . *so that* they could change their family trees for generations to come . . . *so that* they could retire with dignity and leave legacies . . . *so that* they could become outrageous givers and change their communities. Most people, though, only saw the emphasis on debt. They never noticed the *so that*—until now.

About fifteen years ago, two critical things happened in our company. First, we started noticing all the new millionaires who had come around us. These were normal, everyday, run-of-the-mill families who had gotten out of debt, started investing, and had recently hit the millionaire mark. Second, a powerhouse of a guy named Chris Hogan joined our team. He came from a banking background and began working as a financial coach specializing in high-net-worth clients. Most of his coaching clients had a net worth of $1 million or more. He worked with professional athletes, celebrities, and, of course, plenty of hardworking, middle-class families who had built wealth slowly and steadily. It was a new age for our company, as we were finally faced with the long-term success we knew these principles would bring *and* had the right guy in the right seat to work with these high-net-worth families.

Over the past decade, Chris has exploded onto the national financial scene. He's a best-selling author, world-class speaker, popular guest on national news channels, and number one rated podcaster. As his notoriety and hands-on experience have grown, so has his passion for understanding millionaires. He, along with our entire team at Ramsey Solutions, became intrigued—maybe *obsessed*—by the millionaires we kept meeting. They came up to us at live events. They emailed every day. We got so many of them calling into the radio show that we created a new Millionaire Theme Hour, which has become one of our most popular recurring segments. Over and over, people would come up to Chris and say, "We did it. We put this stuff to work, and now we're millionaires. We never knew this was possible!"

Well, it is possible. We always *knew* it was possible, but now we were faced with the undeniable proof. Chris and our team wanted to take that anecdotal evidence to the next level, though. It's been more than twenty years since Thomas Stanley and William Danko released their landmark study of millionaires, *The Millionaire Next Door*. That book destroyed people's misconceptions about wealth and the wealthy in the 1990s, and we felt like it was time to shake things up again for the current generation. So Chris and our in-house research team went to work, conducting the largest, most comprehensive study of millionaires ever. We cast a wide net, reaching out to more than 10,000 US millionaires. Some of these were the men and women who had built wealth through FPU and our teaching principles, but many were people outside our tribe who had never heard of us. We wanted to really get to know these millionaires—whether they already knew us or not.

This book is the collection of everything we learned. If you want to know where the typical millionaire comes from or what the typical millionaire does for a living, this is your answer. If you're curious about how they built their wealth or what kind of advantages (if any) they may have had, we can show you. If you want to get beyond the numbers and really understand what makes these successful men and women tick, you've come to the right place. But let me warn you: the answers are not what you think.

We live in a culture that has tried to tear down the wealthy. We're told that "the rich" are greedy, unreliable, untrustworthy, tax-cheating, conniving jerks who want to steal all the world's wealth for themselves. Those headlines may get clicks online and views on cable television, but they're bogus. That's not who and what the average millionaire is—and we have proof. This book isn't theory. It's not anecdotal evidence or a collection of stories about "that guy we met once somewhere." This is research. It's cold, hard data collected from 10,000 millionaires across the United States.

I'm incredibly proud of the hard work Chris and our research team have put into this book, and I'm excited to share it with you. For me, this book is proof that millionaire status is possible for anyone. For you, it's a fact-based, research-driven rally cry to build wealth and change your family forever. This book will show you how 10,000 millionaires did it. And if you follow in their footsteps, I know you can—and will—join them someday.

Introduction

The American Dream Is Alive and Available

"Chris, do you really think it's possible for someone like me to become a millionaire?"

I was sitting at a book signing table in a large chain bookstore. It was a cold night in late-January somewhere in the middle of the country, and I was on the last leg of my book tour for my first book, *Retire Inspired*. I'd been on the road for two weeks, meeting all kinds of wonderful people across the country. I talked to people who were doing really well financially, and I talked to people who weren't. The guy in front of me that night, who we'll call Chad, definitely wasn't. I could see it in his eyes: he was beat down, broke, and starting to lose hope that his life would ever be any different than it was at that moment. The thought of actually becoming a millionaire at some point in his life seemed like a fairy tale to him.

"Absolutely," I said. "Chad, I don't care who you are, where you're from, or what hand you've been dealt. *Anyone* in this country can become a millionaire." I'd like to say this guy stood up straight and walked out of that bookstore with a new sense of hope and determination. Although I've seen that response many times, it wasn't in the cards that night. He sighed, took his signed book back from me, and said, "Man, I wish that was true. But it's not." With that, he walked out the door just as hopeless and discouraged as he was when he walked in. To be honest, I'm not even sure why he bought my book. I'd like to think that he read it and used it to start building his retirement, but I'll never know.

Hundreds, maybe thousands, of people have asked me that same question as I've traveled the country teaching people how to build wealth. I'm talking about people from every walk of life, from well-dressed executives to grocery clerks in checkout lines. They want to know if it's possible for "someone like them" to become a millionaire. Sometimes, they catch a vision for the millionaire life and get to work on a plan to achieve it. Too often, though, people react like Chad, shaking their heads and walking away. They buy into the myths about millionaires that have spread through our society. They think millionaires have some special advantage or were born into money and have had opportunities that aren't available to other people. They believe the headlines that say the rich get richer while the poor get poorer. So, they do nothing, sitting there while fear and apathy take them further and further away from where they want to be.

But then, on the other end of the spectrum, I've had the incredible opportunity to meet thousands of millionaires over the past decade. As I travel for speaking engagements, it seems like millionaires are crawling out of the woodwork across the country. The more millionaires I meet, the more fascinated I become with who they are and what the *average* millionaire looks like. It isn't what I imagined when I was a kid, that's for sure. One day, while I was co-hosting *The Dave Ramsey Show* radio program with my friend Dave Ramsey, we started talking about the idea of "average millionaires." On a whim, we asked the listeners to call in if they had a net worth of $1 million or more. The phone lines lit up. We knew there were plenty of millionaires out there, of course, but even we were surprised at how many calls we got and how similar their stories were. We decided on the spot to make the Millionaire Theme Hour a recurring part of the show.

So, on one hand, I was faced with an endless stream of people who doubted they could become millionaires. On the other hand, I kept meeting more and more millionaires. I started to ask myself, *If becoming a millionaire is as difficult as some people think, why do I keep meeting millionaires everywhere I go?* That question got stuck like a splinter in my brain. I just couldn't escape it. Over time, I developed a passion to understand what makes the average American millionaire different from everyone else, and that passion led me into a massive research project resulting in this book.

According to a study from Spectrem Group's 2017 Market Insights Report, there are almost 11 million millionaires in the United States today.[1] That's more millionaires than ever before. That same report, though, shows the number of people living paycheck to paycheck is on the rise, with one in three unable to cover a $2,000 emergency with cash. You may be surprised to learn that even some affluent two-income households are struggling to make ends meet too. What's going on here? How are there more millionaires than ever before *and* more people living paycheck to paycheck than ever before *at the same time*? What do the millionaires do that everyone else doesn't? That's exactly what we set out to discover.

The Ramsey Solutions research team and I recently completed the largest, most comprehensive research study of millionaires in history. The last major research project involving millionaires was Thomas Stanley and William Danko's landmark book *The Millionaire Next Door*, which was originally printed in 1996. Stanley and Danko believed that everyday people—men and women just like you and me—could become millionaires. They put a spotlight on the typical American millionaire, and they realized millionaires lived pretty mundane lives. These were men and women who most people would never assume to be wealthy. *The Millionaire Next Door* radically reshaped our understanding of what millionaires look like and how they behave, and my research team and I wanted to know if those findings still rang true more than twenty years later.

Over the past year, we have surveyed and/or interviewed over 10,000 American millionaires. We targeted people with a net worth of more than $1 million, meaning the total of all their assets, bank accounts, and investments (minus any debts) totals $1 million or more. Most of them (89%) have a net worth between $1 million and $5 million. The rest have a net worth well over the $5 million mark. We asked this group everything we could think of to help us get a crystal-clear picture of who they were, how they acted, where they lived, what they did for a living, where their money came from, how long it took them to hit millionaire status, and what their wealth meant to them.

In the first half of this book, we will examine the most common myths that are perpetuated in our society about the wealthy. We actually asked millionaires to tell us what objections they've heard over the years and why so many people believe it's impossible to hit the $1 million mark. Of all the arguments we heard, three key myth categories rose to the top:

1. The wealthy didn't earn and don't deserve their money;
2. The wealthy take big risks with their money; and
3. The wealthy have a leg up in education and careers.

I'll challenge these assumptions with cold, hard facts based on research. As you read through these myths, many of the arguments will sound familiar. After all, it's what the culture has told us about millionaires. We can't get through one news day without reading headlines about how the wealthy are destroying our nation and how the rich are gobbling up the world's wealth for themselves. You'll be interested to learn, though, what millionaires themselves think about these things. Frankly, they think these myths are total garbage—and so do I.

Once I debunk the main millionaire myths, this book will explore *who* these millionaires are and *what* enabled them to become financially independent. To do that, I'll unpack five key attributes about everyday millionaires that will show you how millionaires act, think, plan, work, and invest. You'll discover that:

1. Millionaires take *personal responsibility*;
2. Millionaires practice *intentionality*;
3. Millionaires are *goal-oriented*;
4. Millionaires are *hard workers*; and
5. Millionaires are *consistent*.

In all, I'll show you from research how *what you think* and *what you do* are infinitely more important to wealth building than *what you make*. The truth is, the vast majority of millionaires we studied are hiding in plain sight. You would never guess these men and women are millionaires. The thing that sets them apart isn't the amount in their investments or retirement accounts; it's their mind-set about money. And you can adopt this same mind-set for yourself. I will show you how.

I don't know where you've come from or what you have chosen to believe about wealth and the wealthy. Maybe you've bought into the negative news that it's impossible to become a millionaire in

America today. That may be why you picked up this book—you want to see if maybe, just maybe, you have what it takes. If that's you, keep reading, because all of our research and conversations with millionaires have led us to a conclusion that will surprise you and give you hope. Person after person told us strikingly similar stories of starting with little (if any) money, being financially responsible, making basic investments over a long period of time, and achieving millionaire status. You'll see many of their stories throughout this book. As you read, you'll discover that these aren't *special* people; they're *smart* people. And the good news for you is that you are smart—and with time and experience, you can become even smarter.

I told you about Chad earlier. He didn't believe he could ever become a millionaire. He chose to believe the myths and lies, and it was easier for Chad to tell himself he was destined for *financial stress* than to believe he could make his *financial dreams* a reality. That was definitely not the case for Sheila. I was on that same book tour, doing another signing in another city. As I was signing books, I heard a *thud* as a book landed on the table in front of me. I looked up and saw Sheila, a thirty-something single mom with her ten-year-old son in tow. She looked me dead in the eyes and said, "Chris, the cycle ends *here*." I didn't even have to ask her what she meant. I could see it in her eyes; she was letting go of her old beliefs and had chosen to change her financial destiny. She broke several generations of poor-me, why-me, and not-me thinking with that one statement. I'll be honest: I got chills in that moment. I even teared up, because I knew I was witnessing something truly life-changing, not only for her, but for her young son as well. I still get goosebumps thinking about it. Today, Sheila is most likely on her way to millions—because she *believed* she could do it.

As we start this book together, I want you to believe what Sheila believes. I want you to believe what every one of the 10,000 millionaires we've studied believes. I want *their* belief to become *your* belief. We live in one of the greatest countries in the world with the greatest opportunities imaginable. If you believe that millionaire status isn't within your reach, my goal in this book is to show you that it is. And if you believe that you don't have what it takes to get there, I'm going to help you believe that you do! My team has talked to over 10,000 regular men and women just like you who have faced the same doubts and fears throughout their lives just like you have, and guess what? They crushed doubt and fear on their way to millions. This book isn't a theory, and it certainly isn't a fairy tale. It's a real-world, research-driven handbook designed to change your paradigm or worldview about wealth and the wealthy. This is how 10,000 millionaires built their wealth, and I'm going to show you exactly who they are, how they act, and how you can join them—no luck, lottery, or inheritance required.

Let's do this.

I am living proof that you can come from a poor family with terrible money habits . . . but with education, hard work, and an intentional plan, you can create wealth and change your family tree. I am a strong believer that you create your own destiny.

—AL, $1.5 MILLION NET WORTH

Chapter 1

You've Been Lied To

I want to start this chapter out with a few simple questions—questions that you may be asking yourself right now. Is it possible for "the average Joe" to become a millionaire in America today? The news talks a lot about the income gap, saying things like "the little man can't get ahead" or "the American Dream is dead." But is that really true? Is the American Dream really dead and gone? Is it available to anyone, or is it something only reserved for other people—rich people? I've asked these questions many times, and I've struggled because there were things I wanted to achieve, but I just didn't think it was possible for someone like me. Growing up, I believed millionaires were born into money—and I certainly was not. As a black kid in a single-parent home in Kentucky, I felt like the odds were stacked against me. My family wasn't poor, but we weren't wealthy by any means. My mom did an amazing job providing for me and my brother, but there wasn't a bunch of extra money laying around. Becoming a millionaire seemed like a faraway fantasy, something completely out of reach for me.

Back then, I thought the key to building wealth was to chase after a higher and higher income. I believed that more money coming in would automatically cause me to build wealth. Imagine my surprise when that didn't happen. The more money I made, in fact, the more things stayed the same. I kept waiting for the next raise, the next promotion—always pinning my millionaire hopes to the next thing. You want to know what the next thing was that finally enabled me to start building wealth? It was a career change in my thirties. I walked away from a growing, successful career in banking and started down a completely different path working with Dave Ramsey. He taught me step by step how to not only get out of debt and live on a budget, but also how to build wealth—*real wealth*—the way that most of the country's average millionaires do it. Dave's information was a game changer.

After I had worked with Dave for a while, I started doing financial coaching, spending my days teaching men and women how to take control of their money. These people started to get out of debt and gain a new vision for their financial future. That's when it hit me: if I was going to teach other people how to build wealth, I had better be doing it myself! That was the shot in the arm I needed to put these simple principles into action, and talking with other families about their money all day every day gave me the accountability I needed to stay on track. I began to do more with what I had. As a family, we changed our budget and made saving and investing our top priorities (after giving, of course). We stopped wasting money and put every dollar to work, building the life that we once thought was impossible. It started to take shape right in front of our eyes, and we discovered a new sense of peace and control that we'd never known. We also began dreaming about retirement and thinking about all we wanted to do. We were slowly becoming the *average*, everyday millionaires that I've since spent so much time researching. And now I want to show you how you can become one too.

DEMYSTIFYING MILLIONAIRES

When I was a kid, I didn't really understand what a millionaire was—I just knew I wasn't one. When I saw a famous actor or athlete, I'd think, *That guy's a millionaire. He can do anything.* I thought millionaires had it made. If they saw something they wanted, they could have it without a second thought. It's like they had a magic wand that shot out dollar bills and made all their dreams come true. They lived on Easy Street, and that was a million miles away from my little house on Simmons Street. As a young boy, it never occurred to me that I could have what they had. A million dollars might as well have been a made-up amount to my twelve-year-old brain. That kind of wealth seemed completely unattainable. It wasn't until much later that I finally learned what a millionaire really was. Once I figured that out, it took a lot of the magic and mystery out of the word. At that point, *millionaire* became less of a dream and more of a goal.

What Is a Millionaire?

I've found the word *millionaire* means different things to different people. There's an emotional component and a mathematical component. On the emotional side, I believe people desperately want to experience a sense of financial independence. By *independence*, I mean they want to know their bills will be covered without them having to work for the rest of their lives. They want to know there will be a day sometime in the future when they can choose not to work, when they can experience full control over their time—without driving their family's financial situation off a cliff. That kind of freedom and security sounds pretty good, doesn't it?

I want you to become financially independent, and I can show you how to do that. This book, though, is about *millionaires*, and millionaire status is more mathematical than emotional. So, what *is* a millionaire? First, I'll say I'm *not* talking about people who earn $1 million a year. I'm always surprised when someone thinks that's what a millionaire is. That's not it at all. A millionaire is simply someone whose net worth is at or above $1 million. *Net worth* is the key phrase here, and—like I said in the introduction—it simply means everything you *own* minus everything you *owe*. It's the total value of all your stuff—your house, cars, bank accounts, investments, and other assets—minus your liabilities (debts). For example, if your home is worth $300,000 and you owe $200,000 on a mortgage, you would subtract that $200,000 debt from the home's value, leaving you with $100,000 of equity in the home. If you added that to the $50,000 in your 401(k), the $8,000 in your savings account, the $2,000 in your checking account, and the $10,000 value of your paid-for car, your total net worth would be $170,000.

So when I say we studied over 10,000 net-worth millionaires in preparation for this book, I mean we talked to over 10,000 people whose net worth tops the $1 million mark. That doesn't mean they have $1 million sitting in a checking account, and it doesn't mean they have $1 million annual income; it means that the total value of everything they own minus what they owe is more than $1 million. The majority of them, as we'll see later, have most of their money in basic investments like a company 401(k). Of course, most have already paid off their home mortgage, so the full value of their home is also included in their net worth. Some have invested in real estate, so the value of those properties counts toward their net worth. When your net worth tops $1 million in cash, investments, and assets, congratulations! You're a millionaire. And, as you'll see throughout this book, being a millionaire is more attainable than you ever imagined.

A Farm-Bred Millionaire

Like I said before, I used to have some wild ideas about what a real millionaire was when I was younger. If you're struggling with some of the same misconceptions I was, I think the stories you'll hear in this book will radically reshape your view of the typical American millionaire. In fact, if you were to meet the people we talked to, you'd probably be shocked to learn they were millionaires. They aren't flashy or highbrow; they're regular people with normal jobs, often with humble backgrounds. They're people like Rob.

EVERYDAY MILLIONAIRE

Rob grew up on a farm in western Canada. His father was a professional farmer who raised dairy and grew produce. Wait a minute—am I saying a millionaire had parents who were simple *farmers*? That's right. In fact, you're going to see that several of the millionaires featured in this book come from farm backgrounds. Remember, these aren't trust-fund babies; they're normal people. Of all the millionaires that participated in our research, we found that the most common occupations of their parents were sales, farming, engineering, small-business ownership, and accounting. Notice titles like vice president of global operations or chief executive officer aren't in that list. You'll see later that most everyday millionaires—along with their parents—never had job titles like that themselves.

But let's get back to Rob. With a wife and six children to provide for, his father was a hard worker—and he expected his kids to work hard, too. The family always had *enough*, Rob recalls, but they never had any *extra*. For example, Rob says they always had food to eat, but there were several Christmases without many gifts. He got one new pair of pants to wear to school each year, and those pants became work clothes at the end of the school year. Any minute he wasn't in school or studying, Rob was working the farm with his family.

He took this intense work ethic to college, where he developed a passion for learning. Of course, his family had no money to send him to college, so he was on his own financially. He worked hard every summer to pay the next year's tuition bills, and he worked during the school year for living expenses. Forced to manage his money so carefully, Rob developed a lifelong commitment to saving money. Today, when people ask him his secret to building wealth, he falls back on one of the first financial principles he ever learned: basic saving. "If you spend more than you make," he says, "you will never get rich." According to Rob, it's just as important to get a good education. Rob didn't let his poor farm background keep him from pursuing a degree. In fact, his passion for learning ultimately led him to complete several, including a law degree. From that point, Rob enjoyed a long career practicing law and teaching in local colleges.

Despite a good income as an attorney, Rob and his wife always prioritized saving and never spent money foolishly. He kept his cars an unusually long time, driving his last one for more than twenty years. Before any purchase, Rob has always asked himself, *Do I really need this?* If the answer is no, he doesn't buy it. That kind of financial discipline has enabled Rob to amass a fortune of more than $3.5 million throughout his working life. This is something he thinks anyone can do if they set their minds to it and avoid the two sins that he says steal people's wealth-building potential: trying to keep up with their neighbors and waiting too late to start saving for retirement. "I never excused my spending by saying, 'I'm only young once,'" he explains. "Instead, I said, 'I'm only going to be old once—and I want to enjoy it.'"

Throughout his career, Rob built his wealth through simple, commonly available investments. He took advantage of his company's investing plan as soon as it became available, and he put the rest of his investing dollars into retirement plans and mutual funds. He never received an inheritance either. Every dollar of his fortune is the result of his own hard work, careful planning, and financial discipline. That's a recipe he says anyone can use to become a millionaire.

No Excuses

I love stories like Rob's, mainly because they destroy most people's views of the stereotypical millionaire. Can you picture Rob sitting back while a team of servants waits on him hand and foot? I can't. This guy works hard. He doesn't throw his money around and "flash cash" just for the sake of it, either. Do you think he would have reached that level of success if he didn't have the financial discipline to save his money instead of waste it on new cars and giant houses only meant to impress other people? No way. Rob is the definition of a self-made man. The only inheritance he received from his parents was a work ethic that would put most of us to shame. He threw hard work, education, financial discipline, sacrifice, and patience into a Crock-Pot, and now he's enjoying the rewards that cooked up slowly and steadily over time. And that, my friend, is something you can do, too.

Listen, there is absolutely no reason why someone with the right information shouldn't retire with at least $1 million in net worth. It doesn't matter where you live or what you do. It doesn't matter what your parents have or don't have. It doesn't matter if you'll get an inheritance or not. Those are all excuses broke people use to explain why they aren't winning. Your wealth-building potential comes down to one—and only one—person, and that's you. If you want to become a millionaire, you're the only one who can make it happen. You just have to be willing to stop making excuses and start making progress.

SO WHAT'S THE PROBLEM?

If someone like Rob can become a millionaire in this country, then why isn't everyone retiring with millions in their retirement accounts? I think it's a matter of belief. People like me and Rob will tell you that it's possible for you to become a millionaire, but our voices may be drowned out by all the fear, myths, and lies that you hear everywhere else. We doubt that we have what it takes. Then we let that doubt shake our confidence and influence our belief in ourselves. And like Henry Ford once said, "Whether you think you can, or you think you can't—you're right." My goal in this book is to help you believe you can do this by showing you, from research, how other millionaires have done it.

Fighting Fear and Lies

The world around you doesn't want you to know that becoming a millionaire is possible. We've been told lies about who millionaires are, how they act, and how they got their money. We've been told that the average millionaire has had everything handed to them on a silver platter. We've seen how Hollywood portrays the wealthy, and it leaves a sick feeling in our stomachs. We are bombarded with headlines every day that try to convince us the wealthy are the enemies of the middle class. We're told that the rich get richer off the backs of the poor. We're sold a bill of goods that entitlement programs, tax relief, Social Security, and government-run health care will take care of us. And, it seems like the younger you are, the more likely you are to believe this garbage. For example, we found that 74%—almost three out of four—of millennials believe millionaires inherited all their wealth. That's significantly more than the 52% of baby boomers who believed it. The truth is, they're both

74% of millennials and **52%** of baby boomers believe millionaires inherited all their wealth.

wrong—*way* wrong. Only 21% of millionaires received any inheritance *at all*, and only 16% inherited more than $100,000. But wait. Let's go further. Only 3% of millionaires received an inheritance at or above $1 million. Think about that: 74% of millennials believe millionaires inherited their millions, but the vast majority of millionaires either didn't get *any* inheritance at all or certainly didn't get enough to make them millionaires!

We'll dig into the research more in the next chapter, but what accounts for this huge gap between belief and reality? It's because of all the lies we hear that are intended to make us feel better about our own situations. Listen, if you feel stuck and you're not hitting your financial goals, I don't *want* anything or anyone to make you feel better about it. I want you to get fired up about *changing* it!

We also hear all these messages about how terrible rich people are. Wealth—and the pursuit of wealth—is somehow looked down upon, as though everyone striving to build wealth is doing something wrong. We see headlines that highlight what some rich, greedy jerk has done, and we get confused. We start to think that "rich" is the problem and give the "greedy jerk" part a pass. Why? If someone's a greedy jerk, it doesn't matter how much money they have. They aren't giving the wealthy a bad name; they're giving themselves a bad name! I don't want you to become a greedy jerk, but I do want you to become wealthy. You, like Bill Gates and Warren Buffet, can put your wealth to work for good causes. You can make this world—and your neighborhood—a better place for everyone. By building wealth and using it responsibly, you can fight back against the lies the world is telling people about the wealthy.

All of these things work together to create a distorted picture of what the typical American millionaire looks like. We've taken what we've seen in movies and in the news and turned those untruths and half-truths into several myths about millionaires. Then, we fall back on these myths as excuses for why we can't do it, won't do it, and shouldn't do it. The problem is, though, that a lot of people are doing it—and they don't look, sound, or act like what you'd expect. Instead, they're like Karen and Walter, a millionaire couple we talked to from the West Coast.

EVERYDAY MILLIONAIRES

Neither Karen nor Walter came from money; in fact, both of their families struggled to make ends meet when they were young. Karen's parents worked to support their own family of five as well as Karen's father's mother and sister. Those expenses taxed Karen's dad's salary from the post office and Karen's mom's income as a nurse, but Karen says she was never without the essentials like food and clothes. Walter, on the other hand, grew up in an especially poor home, and he went to work at age fourteen to help support his family. Despite the financial struggles, both families impressed the importance of giving on their children. In fact, Karen said her parents gave her two checks every birthday. One check was for Karen to write to herself to purchase something she wanted. The other check was for Karen to write out to a charity of her choice. This powerful lesson turned her into a lifelong giver and always ensured Karen had a heart of gratitude no matter how much money she had.

Walter and Karen were high school sweethearts and dated for years while they both completed college and graduate degrees. With little family financial support, the pair still managed to avoid student loans, paying for school with cash, grants, and scholarships. This set them up to win big-time as they launched into their careers. Karen got a job in health administration and Walter began his career as a CPA. Having grown up with so little, both were naturally frugal and never got caught up in the need to impress other people. They lived simple but fulfilling lives, making giving a priority, avoiding all debt except a mortgage, and raising their two children with a firm understanding of how to manage money.

The couple took advantage of company retirement plans as soon as they started working. That early start, they say, was the main factor that led to their wealth today. Walter and Karen never received an inheritance, never lived a flashy life, never bought more than they needed, never spent more than they made, and always made giving and saving their top priorities. Along the way, they paid off their mortgage more than ten years early, sent two kids to college debt-free, bought a condo for their kids to live in while in college, and invested consistently throughout their entire careers. Today, all that hard work has paid off, as the couple is sitting on a net worth of $6.1 million.

"I don't think our kids realize what we're worth," Karen says. "We don't even consider ourselves wealthy." That's something we heard over and over again from the millionaires we studied. Despite the myths you hear and the depictions you see on TV, most millionaires are low-key, keeping their wealth under the radar. Walter and Karen don't need to flash their wealth to impress other people, and they aren't in a race to spend it all before they die. Instead, they're doing what they've always done—taking care of their families, giving to causes they care about, and investing their time into local charities. They also remain committed to their marriage, spending three to four months a year traveling and experiencing the world together.

Typical millionaires—people like Walter and Karen—aren't trying to keep up with anyone else, and they don't care about impressing people. They're just living their lives, taking care of themselves and their families, and quietly serving other people. That's why most of their neighbors would be shocked to learn how wealthy they are. They don't fit the mold of what society tells us millionaires look like.

A Race You Can Win

If you believe you could never become a millionaire, then you will always prove yourself right. You'll never save enough or work hard enough to overcome that core conviction. However, if you open yourself up to the possibility—the *probability*—that a $1 million net worth is within your reach, then you'll already be halfway to the goal. Your success will follow your beliefs; it's up to you to decide where you want to go. You have to believe that you have what it takes—because you do.

Of course, if you set your goals toward millionaire status, there will be plenty of people who will try to convince you it can't be done. They'll explain all the reasons why someone like you can't become a millionaire. I've got a trick for dealing with people like that. It's a secret that I use to make them disappear. It's easy to remember too. In fact, it's just three little words: *prove them wrong*. When the world tells you that you can't do it, don't believe it for a second. Just put all your effort and work into proving them wrong.

A great example of this is the late Roger Bannister, the first man in history to run a mile in under four minutes. Up to then, many people widely believed that such a feat was impossible, that human beings simply could not run that fast. Some even believed someone's heart could explode from the effort! Roger Bannister didn't listen. He chose to follow his own beliefs and reject the other voices. Then, on May 6, 1954, Bannister made history by completing the mile in 3:59.4 minutes. And guess what? It didn't kill him. His belief that he *could* do it enabled him to overcome the naysayers and "experts" who said it couldn't be done. That's not all, though. Six weeks later, someone else broke Bannister's record. No one had ever broken the four-minute mile before, but now two different people had done it within weeks of each other. Today, more than sixty years later, the one-mile record has dropped all the way down to 3:43. All it took was one man saying, "I can do this. I *will* do this." Once he proved it was possible, others embraced the possibility for themselves and made it happen.

As I shared in the introduction, there are now almost eleven million millionaires in America.[2] That's eleven million people who've proved it *is* possible to build real wealth in this country. These folks didn't buy into the lie that to become a millionaire themselves they needed to come from a wealthy family or inherit a bunch of money. They rejected the voices that said it couldn't be done, and they made it happen. That's great news for you, for me, for all of us! You don't need a rich family. You aren't out there against impossible odds. Eleven million people have gone before you, blazing a trail and busting the myths and lies that want to hold you back. This is a race you can win.

And, by the way, when you get there, don't apologize for winning. Don't feel bad about your success; enjoy it! Too many people are afraid of building wealth. They act like they don't deserve it and feel guilty for achieving more than someone else. That kind of false guilt is a foreign concept to most millionaires who fought their way to the top through hard work and sacrifice. You see, the millionaires we studied believe something that many people today would find revolutionary: they unapologetically believe winning is better than losing. They aren't ashamed of their success. In all the interviews our team conducted, we didn't find anyone who apologized for building wealth. In fact, they were all proud of themselves—and they should be. They've done an incredible job building fortunes that will not only change their lives but also change several generations of their families. That's definitely what I call winning.

Winning is never a bad thing. Everyone would admit they want to win, and nobody would say they would prefer to lose. When my sons were younger, Brock—the most competitive of the bunch—came off the football field with his head down. His team had just lost 55 to 10, and it hurt. He spent the whole drive home in silence. When we got home, he got out and walked up to his room. Ten minutes later, this kid still hadn't said a word. I'll usually give my boys ten minutes or so to pout, but after that, it's time to talk. So I went up to his room, trying to give him some comfort but also making sure he wasn't being a sore loser. Finally, he looked up at me and said, "Daddy, I think I *hate* losing more than I *love* winning."

The weight of that statement pressed down on me over the next several days. I realized I felt the exact same way. I hate to lose. I want to win. I want to win *every time*. But do I win every time? No. Does that stop me from trying? Absolutely not. I turn those setbacks into *setups* to push me further the next time. That's exactly what the millionaires we studied do, too. They didn't let their humble beginnings stop them from winning. They didn't give up when things got hard. They put their heads down and fought through it, and they came out the other side victorious. That's what winners do, and there's nothing wrong with winning as long as you play the game with integrity.

BUSTING THE MILLIONAIRE MYTHS

Let me be clear: anyone who tells you that you can't become a millionaire over time is lying to you. They may not know they're lying, but they are. They've probably just bought into the doubt and rhetoric themselves. They can't admit it's possible for *you* without admitting it's possible for *them* too—and doing that would immediately make them face their own financial failures. It's easier to believe something is impossible than to get to work making it happen. So, these people simply perpetuate the same myths and misbeliefs that were handed down to them.

I am fed up with the steady diet of lies our culture is force-feeding us about what it means to be a millionaire. It's time to break that cycle and bust through these millionaire myths once and for all. In the next few chapters, I'm going to walk you through the three most prevalent myth categories about millionaires that came up during our study. Using research and firsthand accounts from everyday millionaires, we'll examine whether or not the average millionaire actually earned or deserved their wealth, if millionaires really take huge risks with their money, and if millionaires had an unfair advantage in their education or careers. By looking past the assumptions and examining the truth behind these myths, I'm going to show you that you—*yes, you*—can be a future millionaire.

Now, let's bust some myths.

Millionaires Do

- *Believe they can become millionaires.*

- *Reject the voices that say it can't be done.*

- *Put their heads down, get to work, and make it happen.*

Millionaires Don't

- *Believe the popular lies about the wealthy.*

- *Care about impressing other people.*

- *Let their humble beginnings stop them from winning.*

- *Give up when things get hard.*

I believe that perseverance, hard work, and commitment lead to success. I got married as a teenager and have since raised a family, gone to college, chased my career around the US, and become successful. Our children and family recognize that nothing was given to us and that the above traits will bring success. There is no such thing as good luck or bad luck—only good planning or poor planning.

—SUE, $2.5 MILLION NET WORTH

Chapter 2

Millionaire Myth:

The Wealthy Didn't Earn and Don't Deserve Their Money

"Look at him. I bet he's never worked a day in his life."

I hear statements like that all the time—in the news I read, on the shows I watch, and from the people I meet, and I bet you have, too. It drives me crazy when people make snap judgments about strangers. I remember a time when this kind of thoughtless rhetoric was directed at the poor or the homeless. Nowadays, though, it seems like people are more likely to fling baseless insults and assumptions at the wealthy. They see someone who is winning, and their first reaction is to think, *Look at Daddy's little princess. Must be nice to have such rich parents.* Or maybe, *Those hands have never done an honest day's work.* Thinking these things is bad enough, but it absolutely drives me crazy when someone actually says something like that out loud. When someone I know goes off on a little tantrum about how "easy" rich people have it, I get both irritated and frustrated! To me, it's the worst form of whining, and I don't have time for it in my life—and neither do you.

Statements like these perpetuate one of the most annoying, flat-out-false myths I've ever heard about wealthy people: that they've had everything handed to them. This myth is based on jealousy, envy, and ignorance, and you've got to get past those things if you want to join the millionaire ranks yourself. If someone sees a wealthy person driving a Tesla, for example, it's a lot easier to assume the owner came from a wealthy family than to think about how hard the other person must have worked and how much they sacrificed to be able to afford a $100,000 car. That's the thing about millionaire myths: When we're faced with someone else's success, it makes us think about why we *can't* do it instead of how the other person *did* do it. To make ourselves feel better, we make excuses like, "I can't be a millionaire. I wasn't born with a silver spoon in my mouth." Well, guess what? Neither was I. And neither were the vast majority of millionaires in this country. They weren't looking for a handout; their hands were too busy working. The idea that wealthy people have had everything handed to them is a myth, and it's one we need to debunk once and for all.

MYTH 1: WEALTHY PEOPLE INHERITED ALL THEIR MONEY

TRUTH: 79% of millionaires received zero inheritance, meaning only 21% received any inheritance at all. 84% received $0 to $100,000, which means that 84% of millionaires did not receive enough inheritance to make them millionaires.

Have you ever heard the term *celebutante*? It's a mashup of the words *celebrity* and *debutante* that the entertainment media industry came up with. They use it to describe someone who is famous for being famous. That is, these are people who haven't personally done much, but who are rich and famous anyway. Reality television is littered with men and women like this. Everyone seems to know who they are. The funny thing is, no one really knows why. And yet, there they are, clogging my social media news feed and screaming for my attention on television. This really bugged me early in my career. I was working my tail off trying to provide for my family, and yet I saw all these social media stars raking in money hand over fist. For a hard-charging, hardworking guy like me, it was a little frustrating.

My perspective has changed over the years, though. What ticks me off *these* days is that people actually believe this ridiculous stereotype is what a typical millionaire looks like. They see a celebrity's child and say, "I'll never be wealthy because I don't come from money." If that sounds like you, you're telling yourself a lie, and you're using that lie to excuse your own shortcomings. Excuses won't take you where you want to go, so it's time to shut them down.

The Truth about Inheritances

According to our research, most millionaires are first-generation rich. That means they worked hard, made sacrifices, and lived on a plan. While some people like to believe rich people are just born wealthy, the stats prove otherwise. We saw in the previous chapter that only 3% of millionaires received $1 million or more from an inheritance. *Three percent!* That means if you lined up a hundred millionaires, only three of them would say they inherited a majority of their money from their family. We also saw that only 16% of millionaires inherited more than $100,000. If that is what the research shows, then it's mathematically safe to say that at least 84% of millionaires—if not more—built their wealth on their own! That's without help from Mom, Dad, or their rich Aunt Edna. So the idea that the wealthy all inherited their money is nothing more than a cultural myth created to keep you from winning. Don't fall for it!

The typical millionaire may be self-made, but what about the really, *really* rich people? What about the billionaires hanging out in the upper echelon of society? Surely they're just living off several generations of family money, right? Wrong. The definitive list of wealth in America is the Forbes 400. This is a highly researched, well-maintained annual list of the richest people in the United States. There is a *lot* of money represented on this list. In fact, everyone on the list is a billionaire. That's *billion* with a capital *B*. At the top of the 2017 list is Bill Gates with a net worth of $89 billion. At the bottom are thirteen different people tied for last place at $2 billion each.[3] Poor guys. You may think it takes several generations to accumulate that much wealth, which would make the Forbes 400 a Who's Who of inherited wealth. But the truth is, of all four hundred people on the 2017 list, only 7% benefited from entirely inherited fortunes with no additional effort of their own.[4] Compare that to the number of people who came from nothing—those who were dirt poor and overcame significant obstacles—which represents 8.5% of the Forbes 400.[5]

What does that mean in layman's terms? It means more billionaires rose from nothing and overcame incredible adversity (such as poverty, homelessness, and early abuse) than those who simply received an inheritance from their parents and lived off it without contributing to the wealth themselves. While approximately half the people on the list inherited *some* money, almost everyone included on the Forbes 400 has actively participated in establishing and growing their own wealth. Apparently, the days of sitting back and coasting on old money are over.

These findings from the Forbes 400 and other third-party studies are backed up by what my team and I uncovered in our own research. Let's go back to something I mentioned in chapter 1. Like I said, 79% of millionaires received no inheritance at all from their parents. That means only 21% of millionaires actually received an inheritance. You know what's interesting about this? The Survey of Consumer Finances by the Federal Reserve reported on the percentage of American households who receive inheritances.[6] You want to take a guess at what that percentage was? Twenty-one percent. That's right. Millionaires and the general population receive inheritances at the exact same clip. Don't miss this! Millionaires are no more likely to receive an inheritance than their broke neighbor who's living paycheck to paycheck.

So, what's the secret for these first-generation millionaires, then? Well, the research shows us that it's the opposite of a silver-spoon, family-handout mentality. It's the can-do work ethic they learned from their parents. Eight out of ten millionaires come from families at or below the middle-class income level. When we break that down, 48%—so almost half of all millionaires—described their parents' household as middle class, 27% described it as lower-middle class, and 4.25% of them described it as lower class. It seems that real millionaires aren't waiting around for someone else to hand them a fortune. Instead, they put their head

79% of millionaires received no inheritance at all from their parents.

down and get to work with fierce determination, focusing their energies on long-term goals. *That*—not Mom and Dad's money—is how they build wealth and declare their own financial independence. And this reality should empower you to know that, yes, you too can reach millionaire status.

A Self-Made Millionaire

One of the best parts of my job is the opportunity to talk to millionaires across the country. This is something I love to do when

I guest-host *The Dave Ramsey Show* and when I go to speaking engagements. Pretty much every millionaire story I hear fits the same pattern, and almost none of them attribute their wealth to an inheritance. You'd probably even consider most of the stories I hear from millionaires to be boring. You may think they'd tell me how they invented some new technology or how they rose to the top of the corporate ladder, but those people are few and far between. Most of the time, the stories I hear from millionaires are too dull to get a feature article in *Fast Company*. These are people whose names you'll never know because the individuals aren't all that exciting. They're just normal people, and *normal* people generally aren't that newsworthy. For example, let me tell you about a guy we interviewed in our millionaire research named Thomas.

EVERYDAY MILLIONAIRE

Thomas grew up in the Midwest and started with literally nothing. In fact, he remembers only having two shirts and two pairs of pants for a long stretch of his childhood. He came from a dysfunctional family with an alcoholic father and a mother who struggled with mental-health issues. As a result, he was in and out of three or four different foster homes as a child and both his parents died far too young. Those early years taught him two important lessons: First, he learned that drinking alcohol would lead him *away* from future success. Second, he knew that he did not like being poor. Despite coming out of poverty, loss, and hardship, Thomas had a clear vision for where he wanted his life to go—but he knew he'd have to work for it.

Thomas went to college in the 1960s and graduated with a math degree before being drafted into the Vietnam War. After serving four years, he returned to school to pursue a PhD in math, which he planned to use working for the Department of Defense. Instead, Thomas got sidetracked by a new passion: teaching. He taught math in a few different colleges for his entire career, spending thirty-seven years in education before retiring with a net worth of $2.6 million. Did he come up with a new mathematical breakthrough that revolutionized education? Did he use his math skills to make a killing in Vegas? No. Thomas made his millions slowly and steadily, working in a job he loved and designing a life that allowed him to build wealth on his own terms. What was his secret? He says he always paid himself first, stayed away from debt, paid for everything he bought with cash, worked extra hours, and made wise investments. Sophisticated stuff, huh?

The Best Inheritance

I like Thomas. Sure, his story isn't packed with thrills and adventure, but it's the perfect example of what I've been talking about. Wealthy people are rarely born into money or inherit their wealth from a rich aunt. I sure didn't. Like I said earlier, I grew up in a single-parent, low-to-middle-income household in Kentucky. My mom worked hard, and she made sure that same strong work ethic was instilled in me. As an athlete, that meant I poured my energy and focus into sports, which eventually landed me a football scholarship. I used that opportunity to get a quality education, which led to a good job, which enabled me to turn generations of Hogan finances around. Proverbs 13:22 says, "A good man leaves an inheritance to his children's children" (NASB). That's a charge I take seriously. Today, my three sons have a much different lifestyle than I had growing up, and

8 out of 10 millionaires come from families at or below the middle-class income level.

it's my job to not simply leave them a pile of money when I'm gone, but to leave them with the work ethic and character they'll need to take the Hogan legacy even further. That's the kind of inheritance I want to leave my children.

Your personal wealth or retirement plan shouldn't depend on *someone else* dying and leaving you a fortune. Instead, wouldn't it be cool if you were the one who built a fortune to leave to your kids and grandkids? What if several future generations of your family looked back on you as the John D. Rockefeller of your family tree? It doesn't matter how wealthy or how broke your parents were. Your wealth potential is in your hands, not theirs. I never had wealth handed to me, either, but that doesn't mean I can't create wealth to hand off to my children. Every wealthy family started somewhere. Why shouldn't it start with you?

MYTH 2: WEALTHY PEOPLE
ARE JUST LUCKY

TRUTH: 76% of millionaires say that anyone in America can become a millionaire with discipline and hard work.

Michael Phelps is unquestionably the most successful Olympian in history. Now retired, he brought home more Olympic medals than any other athlete in any sport. He started his Olympic career at age fifteen in 2000, when he became one of the youngest males to ever make the Olympic team. He didn't medal that year, but he made a big splash, so to speak, on the international swimming scene. In the 2004, 2008, 2012, and 2016 Summer Games, with a little more experience under his belt, Phelps was unstoppable. He racked up medal after medal in several different swimming events. In all, Phelps brought home twenty-eight medals—twenty-three of which are gold—before retiring from Olympic competition. Most swimmers competing against him over the past fifteen years probably hit the pool just hoping to come in second.

The thing that's really interesting about Michael Phelps isn't just his success; it's the fact that he was *made* to swim. I don't mean that metaphorically; I mean his body is custom-engineered for swimming. I've seen research breaking down his physical advantages, and it's crazy. His arms are longer and his hands are larger than average, enabling him to move more water with each stroke. His feet are bigger than average for his height, giving him a 10% advantage with each kick. He has a disproportionately long torso compared to his legs. His chest is double-jointed. His lung capacity is off the charts.[7] Like fellow gold-medal swimmer Rowdy Gaines said, "If you're putting together a human being from science, this is what you want."

It would be easy to write Phelps off as *lucky*, attributing all his success to genetic factors that he was born with. And, while all those genetic advantages make him a powerful force in the water, they wouldn't mean a thing if he didn't put in the work to earn his wins. Before he retired, Phelps practiced up to six hours a day, six days a week, during peak training times. He swam nearly fifty miles a week. He had a rigorous weight-lifting routine. He had one of the most challenging nutritional plans of any athlete, consuming twelve thousand calories a day. He prioritized rest and recovery. He would write his goals down and put them where he could see them every day.[8, 9] For nearly twenty years, this man spent all day, every day thinking about and fine-tuning his body for swimming. Sure, he has some genetic advantages, but none of those things would have mattered if he hadn't worked—and worked *hard*—for his success.

Some people, though, overlook how hard Michael Phelps worked to be the best in his sport. They think his winning streak was based on nothing but luck because of his genetic makeup. That's how a lot of people see millionaires too. They think the typical millionaire just dove into a pile of money with no hard work, no plan, and no effort. They chalk it up to luck or the lottery. That idea—the notion that wealthy people are simply lucky lottery winners, married into money, or have some genetic advantage that normal people don't have—is a myth, and it's one that will keep you from ever becoming a millionaire yourself if you believe it.

Waiting for Lightning to Strike

The myth that millionaires are simply *lucky* takes a lot of different forms, but they all come down to one main idea: obtaining wealth is random. People view wealth like lightning strikes, as though they have no control over when and where the million-dollar lightning bolt will strike next. They say things like, "Only special people strike it rich. Not me." They think the only way to build wealth from nothing is to marry into money or invent the next iPhone. Since wealth is random, they see the lottery as a valid strategy. Hey, if building wealth is simply a game of chance, why not? Even if they don't play Powerball or Mega Millions, they may believe that wealth comes down to a *DNA lottery*, a random mix of intellectual or physical advantages that enables only *some* people to become famous actors, athletes, models, or inventors. I think every one of these things is an excuse. It's easier to believe that wealth is random—and, therefore, unattainable for *normal* people—than to hunker down and go about the hard work of building wealth.

Our research has found that most millionaires are self-made. That is, they started with nothing, worked hard using the principles and attributes I'll discuss later in this book, and built wealth over time. That's the long road, though. When I sit down with someone and show them how they, too, can become a millionaire, I often see a flash of defeat wash over the person's face. People usually don't want to hear about a twenty-year plan for building wealth. They want to take a shortcut, and they've convinced themselves that's how most millionaires made their money. They've come to believe millionaires get their wealth through luck, lottery, marriage, or special advantages, and they use that belief to excuse their own lack of effort. Why even try to build wealth if you don't think you're one of the "special" people?

Listen, I want you to get to that point of million-dollar net worth, and I'm going to show you that you have what it takes to win. But just know, sitting around and dreaming about ways to *luck* yourself into wealth is a lot easier than focusing on how to work your way into wealth. The thing is, what looks like luck to the outside world is usually the result of years—probably decades—of hard work. This isn't a new misperception, either. Two thousand years ago, the Roman philosopher Seneca observed, "Luck is what happens when preparation meets opportunity." My friend and mentor Dave Ramsey has a more down-home spin on this. He likes to joke, "I've been working my tail off for twenty-five years, but now I'm an 'overnight' success!" The problem is that people don't recognize the time and energy most millionaires put into building wealth. And forget the stereotypical "rich" entrepreneur or celebrity. Let's make it more personal. I want you to picture your next-door neighbors, just a regular couple with regular jobs in a regular house on a regular street. Nothing fancy about them. They wear jeans, drive old cars, have kids in public school, and do their own yardwork. Got the image in your head? Now, imagine finding out that this couple has $3 million in their retirement account. What would be your first thought? Would you think about how they built their wealth slowly over time, or would you assume they had just received a big inheritance, filed a groundbreaking patent, or won a court settlement because of a random accident? Most people, in my experience, would assume there was a lightning-strike moment for the couple rather than thinking their wealth was the result of many years of discipline. One of these start-from-nothing, decades-in-the-making millionaires we talked to was Sandra, a retired police officer from Southern California.

EVERYDAY MILLIONAIRE

Sandra grew up in a stable two-income household, but her family certainly wasn't rich. Her father was a foreman for a county library department, and her mother was a newspaper proofreader. She describes her family back then as having *just enough* to meet their needs. They had one car, they didn't go out to eat often, and her parents had perfected the art of frugality. Sandra even remembers the family making their own Christmas ornaments one year to save money. She says her parents' approach to finances had a huge impact on her and gave her a lifelong commitment to frugal spending and long-term saving. Those two habits have served her very, very well.

Sandra began her career as a beat cop in the 1960s, and she worked her way up to lieutenant before leaving the police department after twenty-seven years of faithful service. She married during that time, but the couple never had any kids. That left Sandra with a lot of spare time after leaving the police force, so she decided to go back to work. She had a great second career as a customer service representative for a regional airline, where she stayed for twelve and a half years. After retiring *again*, she still found herself bored at home, so she did what she'd always done: she went to work. She started a third career working as an office administrator in a doctor's office, where she still serves today.

Throughout her career, beginning with her early years in the police department, Sandra's lifelong knack for saving led her to invest in tax-favored retirement plans. When the 401(k) was introduced, she dove into it. She found that she had good instincts for investing, and she put those instincts to work in her retirement accounts and some real estate investing she and her husband did on the side. She's always kept her spending in check, telling us that she never wanted or needed to live a luxurious lifestyle. Today, although she's never received an inheritance or started her own business, Sandra and her husband are worth $2.3 million. They've achieved financial independence slowly and steadily over the past forty years. They enjoyed their life along the way, always paying cash for whatever they needed, and now they're free to live however they want in retirement. Sandra isn't lucky. She didn't win a DNA lottery; she worked her butt off! She set a goal early in her life, and she didn't let anything or anyone get in her way. She earned her way to success, and now she's reaping the rewards.

Sandra's story is just one of thousands I've heard from other men and women, people no one ever expected to make much of their lives, build wealth, or retire with millions. But who cares what other people expected of them? Most millionaires I know aren't content with the hand they're dealt—and you shouldn't be either. Instead, maximize every opportunity and overcome every obstacle in your way to reach your goals. That's the attitude that drives the success of the millionaires we studied, and it's the same attitude that will drive yours—if you're bold enough to go for it.

Scarcity vs. Abundance Thinking

As long as you believe that only lucky or special people can become millionaires, you will never become one yourself. You might think of all the different reasons why you could never build wealth, telling yourself, *I'm just an ordinary person*; or *I'm not smart enough, attractive enough, or talented enough*; or *I don't have enough opportunities, advantages, or connections.* Focusing only on your limitations is what I call *scarcity thinking*. It's the voice in your head that says, *There are a limited number of opportunities, and I didn't get my chance.* The opposite of that is *abundance thinking*, which says, *There's enough opportunity to go around.* And that's the mind-set of every millionaire I've ever talked to.

People who are winning financially see opportunity around every corner. They know a rising tide raises all ships, so they aren't concerned when they see other people building wealth. They know there's enough opportunity for everyone, so they aren't threatened by someone else's success. Now, let's contrast that to scarcity thinkers. They only see limitations, usually looking at others' success with a little jealousy and contempt. They walk around with a "poor me" way of thinking, always listing the reasons for why they can't get ahead. They feel victimized, as though other people are gobbling up all the opportunities that would otherwise make them rich. Scarcity thinkers can't see the opportunities around them because they've never been taught that those opportunities are there for *them* too, not just for other people.

If that's you, you've got to change that mind-set right now. Maybe life has dealt you a hard hand, and maybe you've gotten knocked down more times than you can count. I get that, and many of the millionaires we studied have had those kinds of experiences, too. But at the end of the day, you've been lied to. How? People have told you that you can't do it, that success is not for you. You've been surrounded by people who are trying to hold you back. But you don't have to believe the lies; you get to *choose* what you believe. You don't have to be a victim to "victim thinking" anymore. Don't focus on your limitations; focus on all the opportunities around you—the same opportunities others are using to build wealth for themselves and their families. Those opportunities are there for you too. Don't let *anyone* keep you from reaching for them.

EVERYDAY MILLIONAIRE

When I think of focusing on scarcity or abundance, I think about a man from the Midwest named Mack who my team interviewed. If anyone could have naturally grown up focused on limitations, it'd be Mack. He was raised under constant financial pressure. In fact, his parents moved the family almost every year when he was young because they were always looking for cheaper rent. His father never graduated high school, and both his parents worked low-paying, blue-collar jobs. At the age of eight, Mack was responsible for getting himself up in the morning, going to school, and coming home—all on his own. Despite the constant moves and the holes in his school shoes, however, Mack never felt deprived. He instead chose to look for opportunities. That mind-set led him to graduate college and join the Army before starting a long career in the insurance industry. Throughout his career, Mack and his wife lived a modest, debt-free, and frugal life. They didn't get distracted by flashy cars and luxuries, instead opting to save as much as they could for as long as they could. He liked his job, but Mack had his eye on a goal: he wanted to retire early at age fifty-five.

Over the years, Mack was able to indulge in a few things, such as nice furniture and a private school education for their daughter and special-needs son. But through it all, he kept his eye on the prize. He worked and saved and worked and saved. When his company rolled out a 401(k) plan, he jumped in and maxed it out every year. He told us that he never planned to become a millionaire, but one day he opened his investing statement and saw a seven-figure balance staring back at him. He was blown away, mainly because he knew he and his wife wouldn't be a burden on their kids—and because he was happy to have a financial legacy to leave them. He realized he had changed his family tree.

Mack worked a little longer than he originally planned, retiring at age fifty-six with nearly $3.8 million to live his dream retirement life of hunting, fishing, reading, cooking, and gardening. He has a peace and freedom that his parents could never have imagined; more importantly, his children have grown up looking for opportunities rather than accepting limitations. He isn't a celebrity, business wiz, lottery winner, or financial genius—but he *is* a millionaire—technically a multimillionaire. Not bad for someone with vivid memories of walking to school with holes in his shoes. Mack had the same opportunities as anyone else—if not less—and he took advantage of them. You can too.

MOST MILLIONAIRES ARE REGULAR PEOPLE

The research we conducted blows a hole in the idea that millionaires either inherited all their money or got hit by some magic million-dollar lightning bolt. We now know millionaires don't really believe in luck. In fact, we found that millionaires are fifteen times more likely to say becoming a millionaire is about discipline over luck. We gave the millionaires in our study a list of items that could contribute to someone becoming a millionaire, and then we asked them to rank them. What ranked number one, beating out all else? Financial discipline. What ranked number two? Saving consistently. Discipline and consistency. These two factors outweigh a high-paying job, inheritance, luck, and the DNA lottery every time. And the good news

Millionaires report the top two contributing factors to becoming wealthy are **discipline** and **consistency**.

is, we can all choose discipline and consistency. They aren't reserved for special or "lucky" people; anyone can commit to a life of financial discipline and adopt consistent behaviors that will build wealth over time. I can't show you how to strike it rich overnight, but I can teach anyone—and I mean *anyone*—how to become a millionaire over the long haul. The bottom line is that wealth isn't random, and it isn't reserved solely for others. It's available to you, too.

Millionaires Do

- *Build wealth on their own without any inheritance.* 79% of millionaires received zero inheritance, meaning only 21% received any inheritance at all. Only 16% of millionaires inherited more than $100,000, and only 3% inherited $1 million or more. So, it's safe to say that at least 84% of millionaires—if not more—built their wealth on their own!

- *Believe anyone in America can become a millionaire with discipline and hard work.* 76% of all millionaires believe this to be true.

Millionaires Don't

- ***All come from upper-class homes.*** *48% described their parents' household as middle class, 27% described their upbringings as lower-middle class, and 4.25% identified as having lower-class upbringings. That's a total of 79% of millionaires who say they did not grow up in upper-class or upper-middle-class homes.*

- ***Rely on luck.*** *Millionaires are fifteen times more likely to say becoming a millionaire is about discipline over luck.*

I had twenty dollars to my name at twenty-three years old in the early 1980s. My husband-to-be didn't have much more. I never imagined we would become millionaires. Fortunately, I had an employer early on who provided comprehensive education about 401(k)s, and we started saving young.

—CATHY, $2.6 MILLION NET WORTH

Chapter 3

Millionaire Myth:

The Wealthy Take Big Risks with Their Money

"A popsicle? You want to invest that much money into a popsicle?"

In my many years as a wealth coach, I've been honored to sit with hundreds of millionaires. Most of them, as we're seeing in this book, are smart, hardworking, unassuming people. They built their wealth low and slow, managing risk and maximizing their rewards. Occasionally, though, I meet someone with a crazy scheme that they just *know* will double their money. No matter how hard I try, sometimes I just can't talk these wide-eyed dreamers out of it.

I remember one guy in particular. He is a well-known hockey player on one of the NHL teams up north. He'd been on a hot streak for a while, and his salary had grown to more than he ever expected to make. Now, at that point in my career, I thought I had heard it all—but this guy proved me wrong. We had talked about some smart investments over the past year and he had seen his wealth begin to take off, but one day he came into my office with an "investment opportunity" I'd never heard of: popsicles.

"Chris, listen to this," he said as we got started with the session. "A friend brought me an investment opportunity that sounds like a gold mine. We're funding a company that's going to make—get ready for this—*cough-syrup popsicles*! Doesn't that sound great? Kids hate cough medicine, but they love popsicles. This is going to make a killing!"

I wasn't sure I was hearing him correctly. I asked him how much he was investing, and he replied, "A quarter-million. I already wrote the check last week." When I asked him what his wife thought about all this, he told me that he hadn't talked to her about it. When I asked him what the company's projections looked like, he told me he hadn't seen them. When I asked him who else was backing the company, he told me he didn't know.

The look on my face started to chip away the excitement that was plastered across his. I looked at him and said, "So, let me get this straight. You invested $250,000 into a company you know nothing about that wants to make a product most people aren't interested in, and you did it without discussing it with your wife?" He nodded. I leaned back and said, "Well, good luck telling your wife that you just threw away a quarter-million dollars."

Of course, this sports star lost his money. That "investment" never went anywhere, and he had some *serious* explaining to do to his wife. The only "opportunity" that experience gave him was the chance to learn some hard lessons about risky investments. While stories like this can be funny and get a lot of attention, this isn't *normal* behavior for the vast majority of millionaires across the country. If you watched television or believed everything you read online, though, you'd think this is *exactly* what most millionaires do. You'd think they take gigantic risks on stupid investments every day, just lucking their way into enough wins to keep their wealth growing.

Almost all the millionaires we talked to in our research shared similar stories of building wealth slowly, avoiding unnecessary risks, and doing the same simple—almost boring—investing practices over and over across many years. If you want to become a millionaire yourself, it's time to let go of the wide-eyed, get-rich-quick view of investing that leads most people off a cliff. Instead, you need to do what most millionaires do: understand risk, pick investments that balance the risk and reward you're comfortable with, and never get distracted with "opportunities" from people who don't know what they're talking about. Let's dig into all this and bust this myth for good.

MYTH 3: WEALTHY PEOPLE MAKE RISKY INVESTMENTS

TRUTH: 79% of millionaires reached millionaire status through their employer-sponsored retirement plan.

The world of investments is full of different products, vehicles, and opportunities—and most of them are garbage. People have come up with an endless number of ways to creatively lose money, and smart, millionaire-minded men and women stay away from almost all of them. Now, does that mean most millionaires stay out of the stock market, stuff their mattresses with dollar bills, and build their wealth one cookie jar at a time? Not at all. There's nothing wrong with investing—hey, I *love* investing! The problem isn't that investing doesn't work; the problem is that most people don't have a clue what they're doing. I've already written an entire book, *Retire Inspired*, on how to build your dream retirement, so I won't rehash all of that here. What I can do, though, is tell you what most of the millionaires we studied do with their money. It starts with an understanding of risk.

Risk and Reward

The term *risky investment* is a bit of a misnomer. The truth is, practically all investments come with some element of risk—and that's not a bad thing. In investing, risk basically refers to the chance of losing your money. If you're scared of the stock market and choose to keep your money in certificates of deposit (CDs) at your local bank, you're taking on a low degree of risk. Chances are, when the CDs mature, you'll be able to get your money back out. Of course, if the banking industry completely collapses or inflation skyrockets while your money is tied up, you *could* lose money, but it's generally safe. On the other hand, if you're a hockey player making a speculative investment in cough-syrup popsicles, you're taking on an extremely high degree of risk. The stars would have to align just right for you to ever get your money back, let alone make a profit.

Where people start to get confused, though, is by thinking that all risk is bad. That's not true at all. Risk is tied to reward. The more risk you take, the more reward you could achieve. The world is full of risks that we take every day. Driving a car is a risk. Going on a roller coaster is a risk. Meeting a stranger for coffee is a risk. Despite all these risks, most of us still manage to get home safe every night. How? It's because we understand the risks, mitigate them as much as possible by taking safety precautions, and accept the risks in return for the rewards we hope to get.

Millionaires understand that risk is something to be managed, not avoided. Being too blind to risk is like jumping out of a plane with no parachute and hoping for the best. But being too scared of risk is like owning a Ferrari and never taking it out of the garage—you never get to fully experience what you've worked so hard for. You'll only make progress toward your goals once you understand how risk-tolerant you are. If you want to see a millionaire who understands risk in every part of life, let me introduce you to Joe.

EVERYDAY MILLIONAIRE —————————

Joe's been a scholar, a soldier, a prosecutor, and a philanthropist. This guy is a machine, and he's faced and managed all kinds of risks throughout his life. As a teenager, his parents sent him to a four-year prep school. He didn't want to go at first, but looking back, he knows the work ethic and study habits he developed while going through that rigid academic program set him up for a lifetime of success. Not even law school presented much of a challenge to him compared to what he faced in high school!

Joe studied psychology at Duke University before starting graduate school to prepare for a career in advertising. When he realized most of those ad account executive jobs would require him to move to Chicago or New York, and being frustrated by the high turnover he saw in the advertising world, he decided to change his career goals. The Vietnam War was raging during this time, and Joe knew he'd likely get drafted. To get ahead of the curve, he enrolled in a two-year Army ROTC program in grad school. That way, he thought, he'd at least be able to enter the military as an officer. Graduating in the top 10% of his class, Joe could choose which job in the Army he wanted. He volunteered for the infantry, jump school, and eventually the Army Special Forces. He was ultimately wounded in combat and released from the Army on a medical discharge.

When Joe returned home, he took advantage of the Army's G.I. Bill to pursue a law degree. He began his law career as a prosecutor for the state of Florida, but the bureaucracy and red tape made it hard for him to get ahead and grow his salary. That inspired him to leave his state position and open his own law practice. Not surprisingly, this hardworking soldier grew his practice and his salary quickly. Through it all, though, he never let his spending get out of control. The voice of his father always rang in his ears, "Invest half of what you make, never go into debt, never spend any money you don't have, and you'll be all right." Joe built his financial life around those principles, and it worked for him. Throughout his career, even when he earned well above six figures per year, he made a practice of investing half his income into mutual funds. By keeping his spending in check and faithfully investing so much over many years, Joe was able to retire comfortably at age forty-eight.

He spent the first ten years of his retirement traveling with his wife and doing all the things he wanted to do. Although he has allowed himself some nice things, those extravagances have been few and far between. His wise money management, in fact, has left him in a surprising situation: he doesn't need to use his massive investment accounts to support himself and his wife. His Army pension, combined with his state pension from his years as a Florida prosecutor and a little bit from Social Security, provide him plenty of income to live on each month. "It doesn't cost me much to maintain my lifestyle," he said.

So, if he doesn't need it to live on, what's Joe doing with his nearly $2.7 million net worth? He's giving it away. Years ago, he set up a private 501(c)(3) foundation to facilitate his outrageous giving. Over the past decade, he's given away $3.5 million of his personal wealth. With no kids and enough money to comfortably live on, Joe and his wife have set a goal to give away all their wealth before their death. Plus, they donate a huge amount of time doing volunteer work through their foundation and other charities. This guy is a hero in every sense of the word. He's given his time, his money, and even his blood to make this world a better place.

Let's break Joe's story down a little bit. He risked jumping out of airplanes, but he managed the risk through expert military training. He risked changing career goals, but he managed the risk by thoughtfully weighing the options and matching his career to his lifestyle. He risked half his income in the stock market, but he managed the risk by choosing mutual funds instead of other, riskier options. He risked giving away his wealth, but he managed the risk by establishing a foundation to properly evaluate charities and the tax treatment on his giving. Every step of the way, Joe faced risk and found a way to manage it. Where others may have seen risks or limitations, Joe only saw opportunities. And he's made better use of those opportunities than anyone could have imagined.

A Spectrum of Investments

To put risk in the context of most typical investing options, let's think of it like a spectrum of investments from low risk to high risk. On the super conservative, low-risk end of the spectrum are things like CDs and bonds. These are generally safe, meaning there's a low chance you'll lose your money. However, they're also low reward, because you aren't assuming much risk. On the other, high-risk end of the spectrum, you've got things like day trading and cryptocurrencies (which I'll discuss in just a moment). With these things, you could make a huge amount of money overnight—but you're more likely to lose everything. That's because the degree of risk is out of control, and the odds of something going wrong outweigh any potential reward.

Plenty of people participate on both extremes every day, experiencing a lot of ups and downs along the way. Interestingly, though, almost none of the millionaires we studied engage in either extreme. Instead, they keep their risk and reward ratios in check by sticking with proven, consistent investments with long-term track records. In fact, the most common path to wealth creation among the millionaires we studied was investing in growth stock mutual funds through their company retirement plans. Seventy-nine percent of millionaires used employer-sponsored plans like the 401(k) to build their wealth. That's right, the boring retirement plan your company probably offers is the most important piece to millionaires' financial success. That's because the 401(k) and other employer-sponsored plans generally provide a way to participate in relatively stable investments, get tax-favored growth on your returns, possibly get a match from your employer, and set your retirement savings on autopilot through paycheck deductions. I love employer-sponsored plans, but don't worry if your job doesn't provide one. There are plenty of other options. I'll dig into investments later in this book.

What about Single Stocks?

When most people think about investing in the stock market, their minds immediately go to single stocks. I've talked to many people who think the terms *stock market* and *single stocks* are interchangeable. They're not. Single stocks are just one option in the overall spectrum of investments, and they typically carry way too much risk for the everyday millionaires we studied. In fact, not a single person in all the millionaires we interviewed mentioned single stock as a major contributor to becoming wealthy, and not one of the 10,000 millionaires we surveyed put single stock in their top three wealth-contributing factors.

When you buy stock in one company, you're basically placing a huge bet on one horse. You're buying a piece of ownership in that company, and your returns will rise or fall along with the success of that company. That can be great when the company is doing really well. I know plenty of people who have made a mint in single stocks. However, I know more people who have lost their money by betting everything on one company. In fact, I've coached many people who had all their money tied up in the stock of the company they worked for. Then, when the company went belly-up, these shocked men and women lost not only their jobs but also their entire life savings. It's tragic.

The worst of these stories came from a man I coached several years ago. He was a great guy with a huge heart. He had been with his company for twenty years, and he was a serious champion for them. The company offered a 401(k), and they encouraged their employees to put their entire 401(k) into the company's stock. It wasn't required, of course, but my friend got the impression that "good company people" should put all their eggs in the company basket. So, this well-intentioned employee put his entire retirement savings—more than a half-million dollars—into his company's stock. Can you guess the name of the company? Enron. This guy lost $539,000 in one day—the same day he lost his job. He thought he was being a team player. What he really was, though, was an unreasonably high-risk investor. Going all in on the single stock— even his own company's stock—cost him everything he had built over twenty years.

When you invest in single stocks, no matter what the company is, you're giving up all control. You're placing a bet on that one company, and there's nothing you can do to control the outcome. Maybe that's why none of the millionaires we studied mentioned single stock as a contributing factor to their wealth. You've got no control over a single stock. It's a bet with way too much risk. Millionaires aren't scared to say no to those kinds of risks. I know I'm not. I'm okay missing out on *potential* gains that could bring *probable* pain. I'm not going to risk my family's future on a single company's performance or the whims of the average consumer. Instead, like the millionaires we've studied, I'll take on a more reasonable degree of risk by investing in mutual funds. That still allows me to enjoy the growth of the stock market, but in a way that diversifies my risk. Instead of putting ten eggs in one basket, mutual funds give me the chance to put one egg in ten baskets. That way, if one basket crashes, I've got nine others to fall back on. If you want to know more about how all this works, check out my book *Retire Inspired*.

Made-Up Money

Single stock isn't the only popular, high-risk investment. In 2009, a new form of currency emerged online: Bitcoin. This started a craze of so-called *cryptocurrencies*, digital currency competing to replace traditional dollars. Bitcoin and other cryptocurrencies can seem exciting, and I understand how cool it would be to be in on something from the very beginning, especially if it becomes the next Apple or Microsoft. But cryptocurrency is the very definition of volatility. Do you even know what Bitcoin is? It's a new type of money. It is literally a new, made-up form of currency that's being traded for goods and services online. No one really knows who created it; it has no oversight, no regulations, no accountability; and—as of today—it has almost no widespread adoption. How many risks can we squeeze into one investment?

A friend of mine got caught up in the Bitcoin craze, and now he's a nervous wreck. He told me recently that he had cashed out his entire 401(k) early and put it all into cryptocurrency. He said he wanted to be "on the front end of something new." Well, now he's on the rear end of something dumb. He's a young guy in his thirties, so he got hit with a ton of taxes and fees for early withdrawal. If he had $100,000 in his 401(k), he immediately lost $40,000 to taxes, fees, and penalties. So this big investment "opportunity" cost him 40% of his money right out of the gate. Now he's watching the news every day with a desperately vested interest in how one of the most volatile investments in history is doing. Oh, and did I mention he's married with *seven* kids under the age of eight? I don't see how this guy sleeps at night! To me, putting your money into cryptocurrencies is a lot like playing Russian roulette with a fully loaded gun. It may be thrilling for a minute, but it will cost you everything in the end. Cryptocurrencies come with almost 100% risk—and that is exactly what most millionaires avoid.

Risking It All on Partnerships

While I'm talking about risks, I want to briefly touch on one that most people never consider. One of the riskiest financial behaviors I know of is engaging in partnerships with other people. I've seen friends or family members go in together on businesses and investment deals, and I've seen them go sideways more often than not. Even if you know and love the other person, a partnership can ruin your chances for wealth building.

A legal partnership is basically a business marriage. You're going all in on an investment with another person, mixing your money with theirs, putting your financial well-being in someone else's hands. You're fully trusting this person to do what they say they're going to do. You're also trusting that nothing tragic or unexpected happens in that person's life, because if it does, that tragedy happens to *you* too. Partnerships most often fall apart due to what I call the Four Ds: drugs, divorce, death, and debt. If your partner, for example, develops a substance abuse problem, you now have an addict controlling your financial destiny. If he or she gets a divorce, you could have someone else's crazy ex coming after a huge piece of your business. If your partner dies, their adult kids may come after his piece of the company, leaving you with second-generation partners you don't know or trust. If your partner buys a ton of expensive equipment using debt without checking with you first, you're now on the hook for it whether you wanted it or not. I've seen all these things happen.

97% of millionaires believe they control their own destinies.

A few years ago, I had a coaching client who was almost torn apart by a partnership. He and a good friend went in together on a real estate investment. My client was in good shape financially, but his buddy was in some financial trouble. The guy with money problems saw this opportunity as a way out, so he convinced my client to join him in buying 133 rental units. They got a blanket loan on the deal, meaning they had one gigantic loan to pay for all 133 units. Before long, my client found out his friend and partner was stealing. Then my client got a divorce. Things got tight and they started having trouble making their monthly loan payment. This was the perfect storm of theft, divorce, broken friendship, and debt, and it drove the two former friends to court. The whole deal fell apart. Everyone lost.

I hate that story, but it makes a point born right out of our millionaire research. A whopping 97% of millionaires believe they control their own destinies. Each one sees his success as being completely up to himself. A partnership robs you of that power. In fact, 80% of millionaires have never even borrowed money from a friend. If they won't borrow money from them, they're certainly not going to go into business with them. Partnerships turn self-responsibility into joint-responsibility, and sadly, the world is full of people who can't be fully trusted. I don't mind failing and making mistakes, but I refuse to be taken down by someone else's failures and mistakes. I, like almost all the millionaires we've talked to, control my own destiny—and you do, too.

> The number-one contributing factor to millionaires' high net worth is investing in **retirement plans**.

Millionaires Avoid Unnecessary Risk

Of the 10,000 millionaires we studied, we found that the number one contributing factor to their high net worth is investing in retirement plans. As we've seen, nearly eight out of ten of them did this through their company plans. Doesn't sound so risky, does it? In fact, it sounds a little boring. That's because it is. Here's what we know about millionaires, though: They understand *some* risk is necessary, but they aren't stupid and reckless. They simply tread carefully, weigh the risk and potential reward, and then move forward cautiously and confidently, knowing that their success is in their own hands. That's exactly the case with Clark, a millionaire that we talked to from the Washington, DC, area.

EVERYDAY MILLIONAIRE

Clark was raised in a suburban, middle-class family, but he describes his parents as having been "terrible with money." They didn't give him a good example of wise money management and, even though they appeared to have a good life, Clark remembers money always being a struggle for them.

After serving in the Air Force, Clark completed degrees in aeronautical engineering and math, and he had a successful career as an applied physicist in the plastics industry. Clark has worked hard, invested wisely, avoided debt, and slowly grown his net worth from zero dollars when he first started tracking it on an Excel spreadsheet twenty years ago to over $3 million today. He stayed away from flashy, high-risk investments and instead maxed out his company 401(k) plan. Once he and his wife hit fifty years old, they kicked things up a notch and maxed out their allowable "catch-up" contributions, throwing even more money into their 401(k)s. They stuck to mutual funds, which let them enjoy the growth of the market without the risks of single stocks. Through all this, Clark knew his financial success was in *his* hands and no one else's. He says, "If I am a success, I can pat myself on the back. If I'm a failure, I have nobody else to blame but me." It's amazing how many millionaires told us something similar. Clearly, self-reliance is a key part of the average millionaire's character.

Although his focus on mutual funds and 401(k)s may seem extremely cautious to some, he sees it as a good balance between risk and reward. He's taken enough risks to build his net worth to millionaire level, but not so much that any one mistake could wipe him out. It's all been part of the plan he set for himself as a young man. Clark cautions other future millionaires not to be too scared to take some risks in their investing strategy. When we asked him what keeps most people from becoming millionaires, he broke it down into two things: playing things too safe (avoiding all risk) and not having a long-term plan. When you have a good plan that you've thought through and researched, he says, you should be able to take some non-fatal risks to hit the goal. However, if you're flying by the seat of your pants or always getting distracted by the next new "opportunity," you'll always be moving one step forward and ten steps back. Successful people like Clark know that's not the path to millions.

MYTH 4: WEALTHY PEOPLE TAKE STUPID RISKS TO GET RICH QUICK

TRUTH: The average millionaire hits the $1 million mark at 49 years old. This is after years—decades, in fact—of hard work. Only 5% of millionaires got there in ten years or less.

As I travel for speaking engagements and media appearances, I get the chance to talk to a lot of people about their wealth-building goals. One question I hear over and over again from all types of people is, "Chris, how do wealthy people get rich quickly? What should I be doing to put myself in the millionaire column in the next five years?" Whenever I hear this question, I can be sure of one thing: they won't like my answer. The idea that wealthy people have some secret fast track to wealth is a myth. The typical millionaire, like the ones that may be hiding in your own neighborhood right now, didn't strike it rich overnight. In fact, if someone earning the median US household income of $59,000 started investing the recommended 15% of their income at age thirty, they'd have over $1 million by age fifty-five.[10] And that's if they never got a single raise! Just doing the exact same thing for twenty-five years would make them a millionaire. Now, most people *do* get raises, and they're able to contribute more to their investments over time. So, if that's the case, they could get there faster than twenty-five years. But it's not going to be immediate.

This example lines up with what we found in our research. We discovered that the average millionaire hits the $1 million mark at 49 years old. That's after decades of working, saving, and investing. Only 5% of millionaires got there in ten years or less. That's the reality of building a $1 million net worth. Yes, it's absolutely possible, but it takes time. People don't want a twenty- or thirty-year plan, though; they want a three-year plan. But that's not how most millionaires made their money. When it comes to building wealth, the microwave approach doesn't cut it. Practically all the millionaires we studied made their millions slowly, over many decades.

There Is No "Get Rich Quick" Scheme

There are a few legitimate reasons for someone trying to get rich quickly, but more often than not, it's the result of impatience, fear, or plain old greed. Even if you're in a solid long-term plan that's working, it's easy to get distracted by a new opportunity or a friend's "sure thing" investment. Trust me, I've been down that road. Back in the late 1990s, a friend convinced me to put some money into AOL stock. Now, I've already told you how risky single stock is, but I went for it. I started with a few thousand dollars, and that doubled quickly. I added some more, and that doubled, too. I was betting on luck—but eventually, my luck ran out. I ended up losing about $25,000 before I finally woke up and got off that roller coaster.

When it was all said and done, I was left scratching my head and wondering how I had gotten so distracted. That AOL mess pulled my attention—and my money—away from the slow and steady mutual fund investments I had been focused on. If I had put that $25,000 into a good growth stock mutual fund instead of risking it on a get-rich-quick stock deal, I'd be $168,000 richer right now. That $25,000 would have grown to about $1.1 million by the time I retire if I had just trusted the plan I was working on. But seeing my buddy's quick, easy returns got the best of me. I thought, *If he can do it, why can't I?*

Building wealth is a long-term play. That's the difference between the words *wealth* and *rich*, at least from my perspective. "Getting rich" just means falling into a pile of money. All the focus is on the cash, not the person. "Building wealth," however, is about a patient, hardworking person's journey to millions. It's about the character they develop over many years of dedication and persistence. When you work for your wealth over years and decades, you'll usually find yourself with the character to manage it wisely. When you suddenly become rich overnight from a risky investment or a lottery ticket, *you* haven't changed at all; your bank account has. That means all that money is now at the mercy of your impatient, risky behaviors. I imagine that's why most lottery winners are broke a few years after their jackpot. They didn't become *wealthy*; they just got *rich*.

Today, when people ask me how to get rich quick, I always go back to their motives. Why do they need to get rich quick? Whose life are they looking at that seems so much better? What measuring stick are they using? Why do they think they need to pick up the pace? People want to experience all the cool stuff they think wealth can buy, but they don't want to work for it. I've got some bad news, though: if you don't work for your money, your money won't work for you. Sure, I want people to build wealth as quickly as possible, but I don't want them to do it in a way that puts everything they've worked for at risk.

Millionaires Don't Use Leverage

Because I'm often on TV talking about finances, I keep my eye on what other financial folks are saying. Usually, their advice is the exact opposite of mine. Just in the past few weeks, I've heard other financial experts talk about borrowing money from a bank to invest in stocks; using a home equity line of credit against a paid-for home to purchase rental properties; taking out loans to flip speculative properties out of state; and loaning your own money out to others to fund someone else's scheme. Are you noticing a theme here? Most of the financial wizards out there want you to use debt—oh, excuse me, "leverage"—to get rich. Like I've said, though, I don't want to help you get rich. I want to help you build wealth. The wealthy people I know don't rely on debt.

The home equity line of credit (HELOC) is probably one of the greatest marketing success stories of the last twenty years. I hear people talk about their HELOC all the time like it was an investment they're proud of. They're so excited to tell me about how smart they are with this magic wand called a HELOC. Let me clear something up for you: a HELOC is a second mortgage. Period. Sure, no one calls it a second mortgage, and the banks selling it certainly don't want you to see it as a second mortgage, but that's exactly what it is. When you take out a line of credit against your house, you are putting your home at risk. You're using it to secure a loan with a bank. Come on, people. That's the definition of a mortgage!

90% of millionaires have never taken out a business loan.

Everyday millionaires—not the flashy rich people you may see on television—stay away from debt masquerading as "leverage." They see home equity loans, home equity lines of credit, business loans, and private lending for what they are—debt. And wealthy people avoid debt. We found that 63% of millionaires have never taken out a home equity loan or line of credit, and 90% do not currently have a home equity loan. So, that means some of them may have made this mistake in the past, but then they course corrected and got out of that mess as quickly as they could. Similarly, nine out of ten have never taken out a business loan. They don't have credit card debt, student loans, or car payments, either. I'll talk more about that in chapter 7.

EVERYDAY MILLIONAIRE

The millionaires I know are like Larry, a retired insurance professional our team got to know during our millionaire study. Like many of the people we talked to, Larry came from humble beginnings. His parents were Wisconsin dairy farmers who had never gone past the eighth grade. They were hard workers who hated debt—and they taught their children to hate debt, as well. Becoming the first person in his family to graduate college, Larry left the dairy farm and began a thirty-five-year career in insurance. Throughout his working years, Larry kept his spending in check, just like his parents taught him. He avoided all forms of debt except a mortgage, saying, "I never buy anything I can't afford to pay cash for."

He and his wife lived well below their means throughout their marriage, making saving money a priority from Larry's first full-time paycheck. Even when he was only making $5,500 a year early in his career, he still prioritized saving and managed to set aside $100 a month. When he got a raise, he increased his savings. When he got an annual bonus, he saved it. When his company introduced the 401(k), Larry maxed it out. He never played around with debt, and he never got distracted by risky investments that others tried to push on him. He worked hard, stuck to his plan, drove old paid-for cars, and didn't pay any attention to what other people had. The end result? He retired early at age fifty-five and has a current net worth of over $4.2 million. Now he gets to travel, play golf and tennis several times a week, visit his children and grandkids whenever he wants, and enjoy long walks and bike rides with his wife. He absolutely loves his life, and he knows one stupid investment decision or car loan could have cost him big-time.

There will always be new investments, opportunities, and strategies that promise the world but will most likely lead you further away from millionaire status. If there's one thing I've learned from the millionaires we studied, it's that shortcuts are for suckers. The long road may not get you there as quickly as you want, but it *will* get you there.

BUILDING WEALTH LOW AND SLOW

The financial industry is full of salespeople, advisors, and gurus who are lining up to offer you advice. The problem is, most of that advice is about getting rich, not about building wealth. They'll tell you that leverage is a powerful tool in wealth creation, that OPM (other people's money) is the secret weapon to unlock your wealth-building potential, and that saving is for suckers. The millionaires we've studied over the past year would disagree. Sure, there are people who have taken those risks and have struck it rich, but many more have gone down that road and lost it all. The thing is, you never know which one of these two people you'll be. "Low and slow" may not be the fast, exciting, or sexy way to build your net worth, but it's what practically all the millionaires we studied have done. None of them gained $5 million in a single year, but none of them have *lost* $5 million in a year, either. They balanced risk and reward with a long-term mind-set, and now they're sitting pretty.

Millionaires Do ————————————————————————

- **Build their wealth through retirement plans.** *79% of millionaires reached millionaire status through their employer-sponsored retirement plan, such as the company 401(k).*

- **Believe they control their own destinies.** *97% of millionaires believe this!*

- **Understand that it takes years—decades, in fact—of consistent investing to reach millionaire status.** *The average millionaire hit the $1 million mark for the first time at 49 years old after years of hard work. Only 5% of millionaires got there in ten years or less.*

Millionaires Don't

- ***Take huge risks through get-rich-quick gimmicks and fad investments.*** *Not one of the 10,000 millionaires we surveyed put single stock in their top three wealth-contributing factors.*

- ***Take out higher-risk loans.*** *9 out of 10 of them have never taken out a business loan.*

- ***Borrow money from their friends.*** *80% of the millionaires we studied have never done this!*

I grew up in the projects and went to public school and a state college with no student loans. I believe we, within reason, are the master of our own fates. We believe we are blessed because of our giving and hard work.

—CHUCK, $1.1 MILLION NET WORTH

Chapter 4

Millionaire Myth:

The Wealthy Have a Leg Up
in Education and Careers

The thought hit me like a freight train: *Am I qualified to do this?*
There I was, about the same age as most of the players on the field,
but they were calling *me* "Coach." How in the world did that happen?

I went to college on a football scholarship and had the privi-
lege of helping my team win a national championship back in my
"glory days." The championship ring on my finger is one of the few
material things in the world that I'd say I treasure. It's not because
I've got a big head about being on a championship team, though.
Instead, it's a daily reminder that I was part of something special,
that I served on a team of other high-achieving players working
toward a common goal. That experience taught me more than I
could ever put in a book, and I have taken advantage of countless
opportunities from my time on the field. One of those opportunities came right after college, when I was offered the assistant coach
position at a school in Pennsylvania.

Throughout my college football career, I had hoped to go pro with the NFL, but I ultimately went back to pursuing my then-life-long dream of becoming—wait for it—an FBI agent. From the time I was eleven or twelve years old, I dreamed of being a federal agent. Sure, my journey has led me in other directions, but I was serious back then. Of course, to become an agent, I needed a master's degree, and that meant even more school after my championship days were over. My former college coach had just accepted a head coach position at California University of Pennsylvania, and he asked if I'd come up to be his assistant. The school threw in free tuition for my master's degree as part of the deal, so I packed up and moved north. I started there as a full-time defensive position coach, academic monitor, and strength and conditioning coach. That opportunity put me back on the field—only this time I had a whistle around my neck and a team of young men looking to me for answers. From the first day, I felt like I was in over my head.

I was blessed with some amazing coaches throughout my high school and college career, and I honored those men. I looked up to them. They were giants in my mind. And now I had a team of young men looking at me the same way. It was the first time in my life when I truly felt unqualified for the task I had been given. I had *played* the game fairly well, but I didn't know if I had the wisdom, experience, and patience to coach others. I didn't believe I had the qualifications other coaches had, so I doubted whether or not I could be successful in my new position. It took a few months (and several wins) before I realized I had what it took to be a good coach—and once I had that confidence, I never looked back.

I think many people look at millionaires the same way I used to look at my former coaches. They see someone who is winning financially, and they assume that person has some special qualification, some trick or training that isn't available to *normal* people. They've fallen for the myth that wealthy people have some specific advantage over others for wealth building, maybe with an expensive, private school education or with a high-paying, powerful job. *Sure, highly paid doctors and executives can become millionaires,* they think, *but not me.* Bull. As I've said several times already, I know for certain that *anyone* can build wealth, and it's time for you to accept the fact that you—*yes, you*—are qualified to become a millionaire. So, if you think you need a permission slip to become a millionaire, here it is!

MYTH 5: WEALTHY PEOPLE HAVE PRESTIGIOUS PRIVATE SCHOOL EDUCATIONS

TRUTH: 79% of millionaires did not attend prestigious private schools. 62% graduated from public state schools, 8% attended community college, and 9% never graduated college at all.

There's a huge myth being perpetuated that you must attend a prestigious private school in order to become a millionaire. That's just not true—not even by a long shot. Now, I'm a huge fan of education. My sons already know I *expect* them to go to college, but they also know why. I'm not under the illusion that a college degree from a private university is going to set them up to win. I believe a college degree's greatest value comes in other forms. Can a private school graduate become a millionaire? Sure. But can a state school graduate with a plan for building wealth do just as well, if not better? Absolutely. Let's see why.

The Myth of the Brand Name

Not too long ago, I got a nasty sinus infection and had to get a prescription. When I dropped the doctor's note off at my pharmacy, the lady at the counter asked me if I wanted the brand-name drug or the generic option. I asked her what the difference was, and she said, "About fifty dollars. The medicine is the same; you'd just be paying extra for the brand name." You see, the medicine in the bottle works just as hard no matter what brand is on the label. That made my decision a whole lot easier. As we take a quick look at education, it strikes me that university choice works in much the same way. The name on the diploma can make the degree a lot more expensive, but that doesn't mean it's more effective.

88% of millionaires graduated with a bachelor's degree, compared to only **33%** of the general population.

The truth is, 88% of millionaires did graduate with a bachelor's degree, compared to only 33% of the general population. Moreover, millionaires are more than twice as likely to pursue advanced degrees than the general population. We found that 52% of millionaires have a graduate or terminal degree, compared to only 12% of the general population. What's really interesting, though, is that these men and women were often the first in their families to go to college. Only 25% of millionaires had *both* a mother and father who went to college or a trade school, and 46% said *neither* parent went at all.

Despite the high number of millionaire college grads, most of them didn't get those degrees from private universities. Instead, 62% of them graduated from public state schools, similar to 58% of the general population who *attended* public state schools but with only a 33% graduation rate. Another 8% of millionaires attended community college, and 9% didn't graduate from college at all. One of those rare individuals shared his millionaire story on *The Dave Ramsey Show's Millionaire Theme Hour*. Bobby called in from North Carolina. He was fifty-three years old and only had a high school diploma. He didn't let that hold him back, though. After working about twenty years for a supermarket chain and another twenty in his own real estate business, he was sitting on a net worth of $4.6 million with zero debt. He said he credits his wealth to hard work, staying out of credit card debt, and writing his goals down. Bobby didn't need a degree from a private school to become a multi-millionaire by age fifty, and neither do you.

And if you're thinking the average millionaire—state school or not—was an academic superstar with a perfect grade point average, let me bust that bubble for you too. Almost half of the millionaires we studied had a B average or less in school. So, if your grade reports had some Bs and Cs, don't let that fool you into thinking you aren't qualified for a $1 million net worth. As Thomas Stanley, author of *The Millionaire Mind*, discovered through his research, "In the real world, economic productivity is not defined by GPA."[11]

Grades only tell part of the story, though. If you look at the total picture, you'll see that millionaires are more likely to be involved in extracurricular activities in high school. Forty percent were involved in sports or cheerleading, the most common extracurricular activities. Eighteen percent were involved in student government, compared to 12% of the general population. Fifteen percent were active in the student newspaper, compared to 7% of the general population. And 17% were involved in academic teams, compared to 11% of the general population. It's clear that, even in high school, these high achievers demonstrated the drive and initiative that would ultimately lead to their financial independence.

The Cost of Prestige

To be clear, I'm not completely against private schools, and someone who wants to go to one and who can *afford* it should. I've got no problem with that at all. However, let's understand what I mean by *afford*. That means the student has the cash or scholarships to pay the tuition and other expenses without student loans and without completely destroying his or her financial life in the process. If that's you, great! Go do it. However, most of us wouldn't qualify. According to CNN Money, the average all-in cost for a private school is around $45,370 per year, which includes tuition, room and board, and other expenses.[12] Let's compare those costs to the average state school. The average cost of tuition, fees, and room and board for a student at an in-state university is $20,090.[13] That means the private school education costs more than twice as much as the state school! For what? The same degree with a different school seal stamped on it?

Of course, grants and scholarships can bring college costs down for most families. The average *true* cost of an all-in private school education is $26,080 per year, compared to $14,210 per year for an in-state degree. There's still a huge price gap between the two, but it starts to make college look easier for most families to manage. I want you and your kids to set yourselves up to win by getting a solid education; I just don't want you to break the bank or bury yourself under a mountain of student loans to make it possible. In fact, spending your first two years at a community college can give you a great start, and you can do that for less than $8,000 a year on average.[14] Plus, some states now offer free—yes, *free*—community college tuition to in-state residents, which means you can get a huge head start on your education while you're working to save tuition money for years three and four at a different school.

Planning ahead and setting reasonable expectations for where you go to school can enable you to earn your bachelor's degree with absolutely no student loans hanging over your head. That's the best way I know to get your career off to a great start and immediately start building wealth right out of school. The bottom line is this: education can definitely fuel your success, but let's not confuse *degree* with *pedigree*. Too many people get themselves into trouble chasing after a particular school's name, location, or even football team. The important thing is the education, not the school seal on the diploma.

Speaking of student loans, I cannot stress this point loudly enough: stay away from them! Don't be fooled by the marketing, either. Sallie Mae and Navient aren't in the *education* business; they're in the *debt* business. That tuition money isn't free. It comes with a price tag that will wreck your life for decades. Getting out of college with $40,000, $60,000, or—heaven forbid—$200,000 in student loan debt will negatively impact your ability to build wealth throughout your life. Because of the power of compound interest, your first decade out of school will be critical to your long-term investing. Sending all your hard-earned money off to pay for student loans will rob you of your wealth-building potential for years. Millionaire-minded people know this. In fact, 68% of the millionaires with a college degree we studied never took out a penny in student loans, compared to 49% of the general population. They understand that wealth building is a long-term job, and they don't want to waste any time with student loan payments. They'd rather do whatever it takes to get out of school debt-free. That way, they can actually *keep* the money they make early in their careers.

68% of millionaires with a college degree never took out student loans.

Now, I know college costs have gone up significantly in the last ten to fifteen years, but that's still no reason to take on student loan debt. Get creative with scholarships, community college classes, and working while also going through school, because taking out student loans to pay for school has a huge long-term impact. Let's do the math. The average monthly student loan payment for someone in their twenties is $351.[15] If that student avoided student loans, started his or her career without that payment, and invested that $351 into a mutual fund every month instead, they'd have almost $3 million by age 65.[16] Don't miss that. We live in a world where most people believe they could never become a millionaire, but they don't think twice about signing up for student loans. If someone only invested what they'd otherwise spend on student loan payments, they'd retire with millions. In some cases, the education someone *thinks* will make them rich is the very thing that puts millionaire status out of reach. This lesson was brought home to me in a recent interview my team did with a millionaire named Curtis.

EVERYDAY MILLIONAIRE

Curtis was a smart kid and was the valedictorian of his high school class. While he had done well enough in high school to get the attention of some "prestigious" schools, Curtis was happy with the full scholarship he received to Louisiana State University. For him, getting a good education without breaking the bank was more important than the name on the degree. He graduated, went on to earn a master's degree, and settled into a long career in the oil industry. Because he had no student loan debt, Curtis was able to start investing early in his career. He took advantage of his company's 401(k) and built wealth slowly and steadily throughout his working life. Because he started saving early and kept his spending habits in check, Curtis is now worth over $5 million and enjoying a fun and comfortable retirement. Though his college selection is more than forty years behind him now, he knows that a misstep at that point in his life could have derailed where he wanted his life to go.

The True Value of a College Degree

I firmly believe that getting a college degree gives you an edge in life and in business, but not in the way you might think. Too many people see a degree from a certain school as a magic wand that will pave the way for their future. They see a piece of paper with a prestigious private school's name written on it as a golden ticket to fifty years of success. They think doors will be thrown open and that wealth will come their way if they could only graduate from *that* school. I don't buy that at all. In the real world where I live and work, a private school education gives you the same benefits as a degree from anywhere else.

Georgetown University reports that lifetime earnings for people with a bachelor's degree are 31% greater than those with an associate's degree and 74% greater than those with only a high school diploma.[17] Why is that? Personally, I think that wherever you go to school, a college degree gives you a couple of advantages. First and most importantly, it shows that you have what it takes to work toward and accomplish a long-term goal. That is gold in a culture full of distractions and half-hearted efforts. Second, a college degree gives you opportunities that you may not have otherwise. If you want to work your way up in an established company, you may need a degree to get in the door. However, if you're an entrepreneur and want to build your own business, this is a non-issue.

Like I said before, I'm *planning* on my kids going to college, and we have money set aside for that. However, if they choose not to or if they would rather go to a trade school, I still know they'll build wealth throughout their lives. While a college degree makes someone more *likely* to become a millionaire, it doesn't *guarantee* future wealth. Likewise, not getting a degree doesn't mean someone *can't* become a millionaire. Remember, 9% of millionaires don't have one. The degree simply gives some advantages. That said, I don't believe college alone will give my kids a *financial* advantage. It's not the school's job to teach them how to build wealth; it's mine. That's why we talk about money at home. Despite whatever education they receive, I know they'll be *smart* when it comes to money.

Educated vs. Smart

Educated and *smart*, by the way, are two totally different things. Educated means you've gone through a formal training program and have completed the requirements for a particular field of study. It doesn't necessarily mean that you excelled in that field of study or that you showed any general proficiency for it. It just means you showed up, did the work, and got the certificate. Smart, on the other hand, means that you not only have some knowledge but you also know how to apply it. We talked about this in the introduction of this book. *Smart* is simply putting your knowledge and experiences to work for you—and anyone can learn to be smart. That's where the rubber meets the road, and it's why the world is full of smart, successful men and women who never stepped foot in a prestigious university—or any other university, for that matter.

I have known many educated, not-so-smart people, and I have known many uneducated, smart people. Between the two, I'll take the smart person—educated or not—every day of the week. You see, if you're smart, if you know how to apply knowledge to gain wisdom, you'll succeed in life no matter how educated you are. But no amount of education will make up for someone who is content to live an unmotivated, unknowledgeable life. Wealth will always seem just out of reach to that person.

Let me tell you what this looks like in a real-world example. I work with Dave Ramsey's company, Ramsey Solutions. We've become a pretty big organization, and we keep growing by leaps and bounds every year. As I write this, the company currently employs over seven hundred people in our Tennessee office. If you count those who used to work here but have since left, Ramsey Solutions has hired well over a thousand team members over the past twenty years. Now, with more than a thousand hires behind us, how much importance do you think we place on where a candidate went to college? None at all. That's right, even though we're a company worth over $175 million and a nationally known brand, we've never hired a single person simply because of where they went to school. Sure, we look at their history, but we're more concerned with *what they did* than *where they went*. We want to see a track record of success. A candidate with a $50,000 degree has the same shot at getting hired as a candidate with a $250,000 degree. I know that because we've hired state school graduates over graduates from more prestigious schools hundreds of times. In fact, some of the most successful people in the company's history didn't have a college degree at all. What made them win in their positions here? It was their hunger to learn and grow and their work ethic. If you have those things, you can win pretty much anywhere. One of the best examples we saw in our research of someone who was both smart and had a strong work ethic is Jack, a millionaire from California.

EVERYDAY MILLIONAIRE

Jack was born right after World War II and was raised in a blue-collar family. Jack's father and grandfather were both steel mill factory workers, and the family never had much money. He said he was raised to believe that most people don't have money and those who do should be extremely grateful and wise in managing it—advice he still values to this day. Seeing his family struggle with money motivated Jack to get a quality education. That motivation paid off, as he was the first in his family to go to college, graduating with a degree in mathematics. There was no nepotism or family money involved in his school selections. He set his sights on where he wanted to go, and he busted his butt to get the grades and tuition money he needed. Not surprisingly, this go-getter got a great job right out of school, but he was drafted and sent to Vietnam six months later.

Jack served as an Army officer during the Vietnam War, and he was determined to bring every one of the people serving under him back in one piece. He did. After the war, he took that determination back into the workforce, taking a position with a large technology company. He stayed at that one company for the rest of his career, racking up promotions and having the chance to try new things every few years. At his leadership peak, he led two hundred and fifty people and managed a $250 million budget.

As Jack's income grew, he stayed faithful to the investing plan he and his financial advisor drafted when he returned from Vietnam at age twenty-eight. Throughout his thirty-two-year career, his motto was, "With every paycheck, pay yourself first for the future." He did exactly that, investing into company retirement plans, taking advantage of matching dollars, managing risk, and keeping a watchful eye over his diversified portfolio. As a result, Jack was able to retire at age fifty with a current net worth of over $2 million. He now spends his days traveling, picking up odd jobs for fun, spending time with his kids and grandkids, and volunteering in his community.

Looking back on his life, Jack knows that his education was the thing that enabled him to change his family's financial legacy. He's grateful for the educational opportunities he had, and he knows those opportunities are there for anyone. If someone from a poor, blue-collar, steel mill background can do it, anyone can. Of course, he made sure his two children prioritized their educations as well, and now his son runs a private biochemistry lab, and his daughter is a teacher. "Education is really important," he said, "and can really help someone build wealth."

Jack's education gave him an advantage in his career, but he had to work hard for that education. Nobody gave it to him, and no one forced him into it. His father and grandfather would have welcomed him at the steel mill, but Jack had different plans for his life. So he gave *himself* the advantage he needed to get ahead. The bottom line is this: a prestigious education may be one indicator of potential success, but plain ole smarts fueled by hunger, drive, and grit is so much more important. And the good news for most of us is that anyone can become smarter—and for free. Books, podcasts, online training, magazines, journals, workshops, seminars, classes, and more provide wonderful, *free* opportunities to increase our knowledge—but only if we put all that new information to work. You may not get a degree certificate for your home-grown education, but the rewards could be greater than you'd ever get from a $200,000 diploma. All the millionaires I know are lifelong learners; they're always looking for ways to increase their knowledge, because they know every new idea they can put into practice will make an immediate positive impact on their lives, business, and wealth. That's true whether they went to a private college or not.

MYTH 6: WEALTHY PEOPLE HAVE HIGH-PAYING JOBS

TRUTH: One-third of millionaires never had a six-figure household income in a single working year. Only 31% of them averaged $100,000 household income a year, and only 7% averaged over $200,000 household income over the course of their career.

If I asked you what are the top three careers where you're likely to find millionaires, you may think about a doctor, business owner, or senior executive in a big company. Sure, those jobs can bring in a big paycheck, but that's not what the typical millionaire does for a living. Contrary to what you might expect, only 15% of millionaires are in senior leadership positions in their companies (vice president, senior vice president, and the like), and only 7% are C-suite executives (chief executive officer, chief financial officer, etc.). On top of that, only 18% own a business. Believe it or not, the average millionaire is a regular man or woman in a regular job.

Want to know what those regular jobs are? When we asked 10,000 millionaires what they did, the top three answers were engineer, accountant, and teacher. That last one blows my mind! Teachers are often notoriously underpaid, especially considering how hard they work and how important their jobs are. And yet, teaching is one of the most common professions among America's millionaires. That's awesome! Clearly, teachers know not only how to work hard but also know how to plan ahead with a long-term view. That's critical for future millionaires.

Only **15%** of millionaires are in senior leadership positions in their companies, and only **7%** are C-suite executives.

As for income, you may think all of these millionaire families earned six figures a year at a minimum—and that would make sense. Remember, 88% of them graduated from college, and education often leads to higher incomes. So, yeah, their salaries are a little higher than the national household average, and many of them did, in fact, break the six-figure ceiling. We found that 31% of millionaires had an average household income of $100,000 or more a year over the course of their careers. If that's not where you are, though, don't worry. Take a close look at the numbers. If 31% *did* average $100,000 in household income, that means 69% of millionaires—almost seven out of ten—*did not* average $100,000 or more in household income per year. Plus, one-third of millionaires *never* had a six-figure household income in a single working year. Don't miss that. Many people working regular, blue-collar jobs fall for the myth that they need a high-paying job to build wealth, but don't buy the lie: a low salary won't disqualify you from millionaire status—*if* you use it wisely. Sure, salary is *a* factor in building wealth, but it isn't the *biggest* factor. Millionaires know that how much you make isn't nearly as important as what you *do* with it.

Salary vs. Value

People sometimes tend to equate their salary with their value. If an office worker makes $35,000 a year, for example, they may start to believe that they are *worth* $35,000. And if this office worker believes that long enough, the thought of one day becoming a millionaire may seem like a fantasy. Millionaire status will always seem out of reach because that person doesn't believe they're *worth* $1 million. That low sense of personal value can grow into discouragement, hopelessness, and ultimately bitterness. They see others enjoying a rich life, but they can't imagine getting there themselves. They say things like, "I don't make enough money to save," or "I'm not qualified to make enough money to build wealth," or "Someone in my position can never get ahead." I can't tell you how many people quit the millionaire journey before they ever even get started just because of this false belief.

Wake up, people. Your income today is not a reflection of your personal value. It's simply a reflection of how much your employer can afford to pay you to do a particular job and how much the marketplace thinks that job is worth. A $35,000 income today doesn't mean that's all you'll ever make. It also doesn't mean you're disqualified from building wealth. Don't believe me? Fine, I'll let the math do the talking. For simplicity's sake, let's say you get a $35,000 job out of college at age twenty-two, and you stay in that same job—never even getting a raise—until you're sixty-five. If you stay out of debt and live within your means, you should be able to invest the recommended 15% of your income, which comes to $437 a month. Putting $437 into a retirement account every month from age twenty-two to sixty-five will leave you with nearly $3.5 million at retirement.[18] And that's if you never got a raise, never saved any extra, never became a two-income household, never paid off your house, and never invested more. With that size nest egg, your annual retirement income would be about five times greater than the $35,000 you made throughout your life! Are you starting to realize that *anyone* can do this? I hope so!

Everyone Wants More

Even though I know practically anyone can become a millionaire over time at almost any income level, I'm not stupid. I know that more money can make it easier to reach your goals. You'll become a millionaire a lot faster with a $100,000 salary than you will with a $50,000 salary, right? Well, maybe—and maybe not. If you're sitting at $35,000 or even $60,000, you may think all your problems would be over if you hit the six-figure mark. Many families who have gotten there, though, have been disappointed by what they discovered. NPR ran a story in which they interviewed several families who earn more than $100,000 a year. Their question was simple: "What does living on $100,000 a year look like?" You may be surprised at what they found. Emma Bowman, who reported on the findings for NPR, explained, "On paper, that kind of salary is considered well-off. But as we heard from many, it often takes just one major expense for that to not feel like enough."[19]

One family they interviewed acknowledged their $100,000 income made them "far from destitute," but then said they had recently declared bankruptcy because they couldn't pay their bills. Despite their high income, they were forced to take extra jobs and admitted, "We haven't been able to do Christmas in ten years. We don't even have a tree."[20] Another six-figure family reported, "It's embarrassing to say that you have to work overtime in order to make enough money to live on . . . working second jobs and even third jobs to try to put together the money just to stay in the middle class where [we've] been in the past."[21] Family after family reported big incomes and the same amount of debt, stress, and anxiety—if not more—than they'd had when their incomes were much lower.

Hearing families whine about *only* making $100,000 can be confusing—not to mention infuriating—to families making it work on half that. Even though these high-income families seem completely out of control, though, I understand where they're coming from. The problem they're having is the same problem I had early in my career: they increased their lifestyles in proportion to their increased incomes. So a 20% salary increase came with a 20% increase in lifestyle spending—and often a 20% increase in financial stress. Think about it: How often have you seen someone get a raise at work and then immediately "celebrate" by buying a new car? Their raise may have been $400 a month, but their new car payment is $500! All that pay bump did was put them $100 more in the hole every month. That's because they didn't adjust their mindset and make a plan for their money. If you don't have a plan, more money will simply bring you more problems. In many situations, more money is the *last* thing you need.

That's why I'm all about busting the millionaire myths and talking about the attributes that will set you up for wealth building. So get your head in the game! You need to learn the ins and outs of handling money, but none of that will matter if you don't change your thinking. If you aren't mentally and emotionally prepared for wealth, you're going to miss or waste every opportunity you get to become a millionaire. Instead, I want you to become more like Brian, a retired millionaire in the Northeast who our team recently interviewed.

EVERYDAY MILLIONAIRE ─────────────────────────

Brian came from a working-class family he describes as "not rich, but not poor." His father was a small-business owner and taught Brian the value of work at a young age. He told us that he mowed yards in the summer, shoveled snow in the winter, and washed dishes at a local restaurant as a boy. "If you wanted money, you went to work," he says. "It's just what you did." That solid work ethic and respect for hard-earned money served Brian well, especially after he went through an unexpected career change in his late thirties. After his employer was forced to eliminate his position due to financial reasons, Brian picked himself up, went back to school, and learned an entirely new field. That enabled him to start a second career at a time when many of his friends were at the peak of their success.

Through it all, Brian never earned more than an average middle-class wage, but he also always kept his spending and lifestyle in check. He knew from his father and grandfather that real wealth comes not from a high-paying job but from solid, consistent investments. So, throughout his entire career, Brian lived on 80% of his income and saved the other 20%—no matter what his salary was at any given time. That discipline, commitment, and reasonable lifestyle enabled this normal, middle-class guy to retire early at age fifty-nine with a net worth of over $2.3 million. When we asked him why more people don't achieve what he was able to, he said it was simple. "The main things that keep people from becoming millionaires are their spending habits and their saving/spending ratios," he explains. "If you save 1% and spend 99%, you aren't going anywhere." I think *ratios* is the key word here. Brian made the commitment to himself early on to save 20% of his income no matter how much or how little he made. By doing that consistently—always keeping his spending and saving ratios in check—he became a millionaire almost on autopilot.

Despite the images that many people have about millionaires, Brian's conservative lifestyle and long-term wealth-building plan aren't that unusual. In fact, that combination of hard work, goal setting, and percentage-based saving is something we saw over and over again in our research.

HIDING IN PLAIN SIGHT

By now, I hope you're realizing the image that most people have of millionaires doesn't line up with reality. Too often we focus on what we *think* rich people have—an expensive education, a powerful, high-paying job, a big house, nice cars, or fine jewelry. Listen, there is nothing wrong with having those things, and I have plenty of millionaire friends who look, live, and act just like that. What I want you to see, though, is that *most* millionaires are hiding in plain sight. You'd never notice them because they don't look like what you'd expect. I'm talking about the insurance agent who sold you a policy on your car, the overall-wearing farmer who you buy eggs from at the farmers' market, and the teacher who works with your kids all day. In fact, from what I've learned in these millionaire interviews, I'd say there's a good chance a high-income doctor is facing more financial stress than his middle-class office staff.

The everyday millionaires I know prove that an expensive education and a high-paying job aren't requirements for building wealth. Sure, I'd love for you to make more money, but I don't think more money is what most people need. In fact, I know from experience that *more* doesn't equal *better* if you aren't ready for it. Instead, the only qualification for becoming a millionaire is a mind-set that makes the most of every opportunity. If I can get you to adopt a millionaire mind-set—no matter what your income is—I know you can build wealth over time. And that'll be a *real* leg up on millionaire status!

Millionaires Do ──────────────────────────

- **Go to college.** *88% of millionaires graduated with a bachelor's degree, compared to only 33% of the general population.*

- **Work for companies and not for themselves.** *Only 18% own a business.*

- **Have regular jobs.** *The top three occupations for millionaires are engineer, accountant, and teacher.*

Millionaires Don't

- **Attend fancy, exclusive universities.** *79% of millionaires did not attend prestigious private schools—62% graduated from public state schools, 8% attended community college, and 9% never graduated college at all.*

- **Ace all their classes in college.** *48% of millionaires had a B average or less in school.*

- **Take out student loans.** *68% of millionaires with a college degree never took out a penny in student loans, compared to 49% of the general population.*

- **All have high-paying jobs.** *One-third of millionaires never had a six-figure household income in a single working year. Only 31% of them averaged $100,000 household income a year, and only 7% averaged over $200,000 household income over the course of their career.*

Belief is key. If you believe you can do it, you eventually will. If you believe you can't, then you definitely won't.

—STEW, $2.8 MILLION NET WORTH

Chapter 5

Stop Making Excuses and Start Believing

Okay, now it's time for a gut check. There's no point in us continuing with this book until we get something out of the way. I need you to stop right where you are and ask yourself a critical, life-changing question. You ready? Here it is—you need to ask yourself right now, *Do I believe that I have what it takes, that I can and should become a millionaire?* That's it. That's the question. If you haven't dealt with this issue yet, now's the time. Go ahead, spend a minute or two answering that for yourself.

STOP BELIEVING LIES

At the start of this book, we established that we've been lied to about millionaires. And I've just spent several chapters debunking the most common millionaire myths we discovered in our research. Let's do a quick review.

- **MYTH 1: Wealthy People Inherited All Their Money**
  TRUTH: 79% of millionaires received zero inheritance, meaning only 21% received any inheritance at all. Only 16% of millionaires inherited more than $100,000, and only 3% inherited $1 million or more.

- **MYTH 2: Wealthy People Are Just Lucky**
  TRUTH: 76% of millionaires say that anyone in America can become a millionaire with discipline and hard work.

- **MYTH 3: Wealthy People Make Risky Investments**
  Truth: 79% of millionaires reached millionaire status through their employer-sponsored retirement plan.

- **MYTH 4: Wealthy People Take Stupid Risks to Get Rich Quick**
  TRUTH: The average millionaire hits the $1 million mark at 49 years old. This is after years—*decades*, in fact—of hard work. Only 5% of millionaires got there in ten years or less.

- **MYTH 5: Wealthy People Have Prestigious Private-School Educations**
  TRUTH: 79% of millionaires did not attend prestigious private schools. 62% graduated from public state schools, 8% attended community college, and 9% never graduated college at all.

- **MYTH 6: Wealthy People Have High-Paying Jobs**
  TRUTH: One-third of millionaires never had a six-figure household income in a *single* working year. Only 31% of them averaged $100,000 household income a year, and only 7% averaged over $200,000 household income over the course of their career.

So, now that we've established the real truth behind these myths, are you still going to believe that you can never become wealthy, or are you going to believe the hard data and personal stories of over 10,000 millionaires? Myths are lies, remember? And I normally don't waste my time dealing with someone else's lies. I usually just hear them, laugh, and move on with my life. But I didn't unpack and tear apart these myths for myself; I did it for you. Maybe you've stumbled over these lies in the past. Maybe you've always believed that millionaires were born into money, and since you weren't, you thought you missed the boat. Maybe you thought millionaires got rich by taking crazy risks or using super-secret investments that aren't available to *normal* people. Maybe you've been held back by the false belief that millionaires are somehow uniquely qualified for wealth building, and you don't think you made the cut. Or maybe you've let the fear of trying something new scare you off. But not anymore—now you know that *you* have the power to make millionaire status happen for yourself.

You see, all these lies make people nervous about investing and wealth building. The stock market, for example, can seem like the world's riskiest roller coaster, and the thought of buying a ticket may freak you out. I can understand that. In the past ten or twenty years, we've seen the market bounce around all over the place. The 2008 market crash left people scared and scrambling. The Enron fiasco destroyed a lot of people's lives. The record-breaking gains of 2017 left many scratching their heads and wondering if we were in a bubble getting ready to pop. Add to that the high-profile scandals like Bernie Madoff, who stole an estimated $64 billion from his investors, and Martha Stewart, who went to jail for insider trading, and the whole system starts to look a little too suspicious.

If you were in high school or college during these ups and downs, you may have seen the frightened looks of your parents and determined then and there to never trust the market with your money. I understand. If I only looked at the past twenty years, I'd be nervous too. But you can't do that with the stock market; you have to look at the *entire* history of the market. This is something I go into great detail about in my previous book, *Retire Inspired*. If you're curious about (or scared of) how the stock market works, you can learn all the ins and outs in that book.

I get it. I've believed the lies. I've been scared to try something new. I've wasted a lot of money on "shiny object syndrome." Seriously, I've been there. But thank God I'm not there anymore. Wise teachers and mentors have shown me the truth behind these myths, and one of my goals in this book is to pass that truth along to you. Now, as we put these myths to bed once and for all, it's time to zero in on the power of belief and what it means for your wealth building. Once I turned my back on the lies and started *believing* I could be a millionaire, the whole course of my life began to move in that direction. Yours can too.

Going against the Flow

In chapter 2, I talked about Michael Phelps and how his body was practically designed for swimming. Way down at the opposite end of the "made for swimming" spectrum is Chris Hogan. Phelps is built like a torpedo; I'm built like a tank—and tanks typically aren't that effective in the water. So, needless to say, I've never been white water rafting. One of the things that keeps me off the rapids is the high current of the water. A friend once told me that he got knocked out of a raft, went underwater, and was immediately shot several rafts away from the one he started in. A group of strangers had to pull him into their raft, because there was no hope of him getting back to his. Another buddy told me how he once fell out and got sucked *underneath* his own raft. He had to push off the bottom of his own boat in order to get free and, when he did, the current sent him downstream like a missile. Sorry, but that's just not my idea of fun. This body belongs on dry land or at least in a sturdy boat with an engine—preferably a cruise ship.

I don't like being at the mercy of a current I can't control. On one hand, it's easy. The current does all the work. On the other hand, you don't get to choose your destination. If you stay in your raft, the river will take you where it wants you to go. And, at the end of the ride, you'll find yourself surrounded by everyone else who took the same trip you did. That's how I view the myths society tells us about building wealth. The culture is flowing one way, pushing us along with lies about debt, credit cards, student loans, home equity lines of credit, and overspending. It's easy to buy into the fear, myths, and lies we hear every day, because going with the flow and believing what everyone else believes doesn't require anything of us. We can just hang on, take the same ride as everyone else, and get the same rewards. When it comes to building wealth, though, the ones who come out on top aren't the ones who merely *survive* the ride; it's the ones who went *against* the flow and chose a new destination for themselves. That's what I want you to do with your money.

Guaranteeing Failure

I can't say this enough: Believing the myths about wealth and the wealthy will prevent you from ever becoming wealthy yourself. Saying *I can't* or *It's not possible for someone like me* will become a self-fulfilling prophecy. You'll be shortchanging your potential and guaranteeing your own failure.

By now, the phrase "someone like me" should have new meaning to you. We've seen over and over again that the typical millionaire in this country is someone just like you. These men and women are regular people. They didn't have special advantages, and they weren't born rich. They came from little (or nothing) and still came out on top. Rob, who we got to know in chapter 1, grew up on a farm and only had one good pair of pants for school each year. Sandra, in chapter 2, grew up in a frugal family who had just enough to meet their needs and nothing more. Neither of these folks were content with the hand they were dealt, so they changed the game. Instead of letting their backgrounds hold them back, these two used their experiences as a springboard to shoot them further than their parents ever hoped to go.

The millionaires we studied didn't have an inside track on some mysterious investment scheme; they simply used commonly available retirement plans. Remember, they viewed the standard, *boring* company retirement plan as the number one contributor to their high net worth. In chapter 2, we saw that Mack, a retired military man and insurance professional, was able to become a millionaire and retire at age fifty-six—just by consistently investing into his company retirement plan. Clark, in chapter 3, intentionally stayed away from high-risk investments and focused almost exclusively on the 401(k) through his company. He retired wealthy too.

The average millionaire also doesn't have a crazy-high salary; he or she just has a regular job. In chapter 3, we saw that Larry retired with millions in his 401(k) at age fifty-five, and he did it by making saving a priority throughout his career—regardless of his income level. In fact, this guy was saving $100 a month when he was only making $5,500 a year! And, of course, we saw Brian in chapter 4, who never earned more than a typical middle-class income *and* went through an unexpected career change in his late thirties and *still* retired in his fifties with millions to live on.

You want to know why Rob, Sandra, Mack, Clark, Larry, Brian, and the over 10,000 millionaires we studied made it to the millionaire finish line? It's because they rejected the myths that told them "someone like them" couldn't do it. They chose a different path; they chose to swim upstream. That's the very definition of courage as far as I'm concerned. Psychologist Rollo May once said, "The opposite of courage in our society is not cowardice, it's conformity." Average millionaires refuse to conform to the norms of society. Instead, they boldly and bravely stand apart from what everyone else is doing and where everyone else is going, and they tell themselves, *There's a better way, and I'm going to follow that instead.* As a result, they're experiencing the thrills the rest of the crowd will never know.

The Skin of a Lie

So, why do some people allow themselves to believe these myths? Personally, I think it's just easier to make excuses. Some people need to imagine a villain working against them to excuse their own failings or lack of motivation. They can't (or won't) say, "It's my fault I'm not winning," so they parrot the same tired old phrases they might have heard from their parents. There's a problem with this fallback position, though. You'll never make any progress as long as you're making excuses.

Back when I played college football, I remember making a mistake on the field and letting an opposing player get past me. My coach, a wise man named Ernie Horning, asked me what happened, and I had all kinds of excuses for why it wasn't my fault. Coach Horning looked at me and said, "Son, an excuse is the skin of a lie wrapped with a reason." As I thought about what he meant, I realized he had given me one of the most important life lessons I'd ever received. An excuse is a lie dressed up as an explanation. It's a way to justify my own mistakes and failures by blaming someone or something else. That's the easy way out, and it comes at a price. Wonderful mentors like my mom, uncles, grandparents, and the late, great Coach Horning helped me realize that excuses will steal any chance I have at success. If you want to get past the myths and set yourself on the path toward millionaire status, you've got to have the courage and conviction to say, *I'm the reason I'm not winning yet, and I'm the reason I will win in the future.* With that shift in mindset, you'll start to see all the wealth-building opportunities that you used to think only came to *other* people—only this time, they'll be coming to you.

Different Starting Lines

I believe we get to choose our finish line, but I also understand we're not all starting at the same spot. There are people who *do* have some advantages working for them. That's just life. Someone will *always* have more advantages than you seem to have, no matter who you are or what you've got. The point isn't where you're starting from, though; it's where you're going. We are all born with the same power of choice, and how we use that power will have a huge impact on our destination. In fact, one of the most interesting things I saw from our research was all the different backgrounds these 10,000 millionaires had. They came from all walks of life and all types of family situations. They lived in all parts of the country, from California to New York—including plenty in the flyover states like Ohio and Illinois. They came from upper-class, middle-class, *and* lower-class families. There was almost an even split personality-wise, too, with 53% identifying as introverts and 47% as extroverts. But no matter who they were or where they started from, these millionaire-minded men and women weren't content to go wherever the current took them, and they didn't feel bound to stay in the same place they started from. Like Clark says in chapter 3, "If I am a success, I can pat myself on the back. If I'm a failure, I have nobody else to blame but me."

53% of millionaires identify as introverts and **47%** as extroverts.

Oftentimes, the problem isn't where we came from; it's the mistakes we've made ourselves. For example, if you're already in your thirties and are under a mountain of car loans, interest payments, and credit card debt, then you're going to have a harder time hitting the millionaire mark. You've got to clean up the mess you made before you can refocus your energy on building wealth. You spent years putting yourself in a hole, and now it's going to take some time to climb out—but you can do it. It's not going to be impossible to reach millionaire status; it just means it'll take longer. Picture it this way: You may have spent the first several years of your adult life running in the wrong direction. Once you turn around and face the right way, you've got more ground to cover on your way to the finish line. Don't use that as an excuse to give up; use it as motivation to run even harder. You can make progress, or you can make excuses. You can't make both.

TRUTH CHANGES YOU

It's always easier to live in a lie if no one has ever told you the truth. When I was a kid, my dreams weren't much bigger than the house I grew up in. As I said earlier, I came from an amazing family, and we always had *enough*. Early on, that's all I thought was possible for me, so I didn't really think about building wealth and moving on from that small town. Then, one afternoon after baseball practice, I experienced an unexpected paradigm shift. My coach took me and some other players home, and he dropped off one of the kids from the nicer part of town first. I remember looking out the car window at the house my teammate was walking into. It was big and beautiful. It had a perfectly manicured lawn. It had nice cars in the driveway. It looked a lot different than my house, and I remember thinking something like, *It must be nice to have all that.*

Then, probably sensing what I and another teammate in the car were thinking, my coach turned around and looked at us in the back seat. He said, "Boys, this life is possible for you." I couldn't escape what he said. No one had ever told me that before. No one had ever even mentioned the possibility of me living in a house like that or having the things my wealthy friends had. It was hard to believe, because I didn't have the advantages they had. But I went home that night and realized I had two options: I could pout and be upset about what I didn't have, or I could start getting a clear picture in my head of what I wanted to chase. Seeing how someone else lived could have been either my fuel or my finality. It could drive me where I wanted to go, or it could leave me sitting where I had always been. I chose to drive forward, and I haven't stopped since.

If you're where I was back then, allow me to do for you what my coach did for me that day. It's my job—and my joy—to tell you that building wealth is possible for you. Will it be easy? Heck no! Nothing worth doing ever is. I never said becoming a millionaire was *easy*; I just said it was *possible*. If you aren't ready to put in the work and take control of your money, you won't make it. If you just sit on your butt all day and whine about what everyone else has, you won't make it. But if you're ready to break free of the culture's lies and step into the truth, you have just as good of a shot as anyone else. This is your permission slip to become a millionaire—and all you have to do is take it, sign it, and own all the responsibilities that come with it. If you can do that, I promise you can get there.

The Truth about Millionaires

When I first started working with, talking to, and studying millionaires, my eyes were opened—and maybe, now that you're a few chapters into this book, your eyes have been, too. All the myths and lies I had heard my entire life started falling away—but things weren't changing for me yet. Then, as I got my finances under control using Dave Ramsey's simple Baby Steps, my vision for *where* I wanted to go and *how* I wanted to get there came into focus. At that point, I fully believed that I could achieve my millionaire goals because I had both the vision and the plan. After trying (and failing) to *get rich* for years, I realized it was time for me to try doing things the right way—by *building wealth* slowly. I knew from Dave and others that becoming a millionaire is something I *could* do, but I had been going about it the wrong way. Once I got the information I was missing, I paired that with my belief that I could build wealth, and I was off to the races.

So, what information are you missing? If you need to learn how to manage your money and get out of debt, pick up a copy of Dave Ramsey's *The Total Money Makeover*. If you need to learn how basic retirement options work and how to put a plan together for yourself, check out my previous book, *Retire Inspired*. And if you need to learn what 10,000 millionaires believe are the keys to blasting past a $1 million net worth, then stay right here. We're going to spend the second half of this book displacing the lies with truth—specifically, the truth about what millionaires believe and what they do to get to millionaire status—and how you can implement those same things in your own life.

You see, my team and I weren't just interested in what these men and women had and how they got there; we wanted to *really* get to know them. That meant going beyond the superficial details and asking character-driven questions. It meant talking to them in person or on the phone, taking the time to listen to their stories and understand what was important to them. Finally, it meant processing all that information from over 10,000 people and distilling it into a picture that truly represents the heart of the average American millionaire. As we did that, five key characteristics rose to the top. These are five attributes that we believe are remarkably consistent across all types of millionaires from all over the country.

By this point, you probably won't be surprised by how simple—even basic—these attributes are. First, average millionaires take *personal responsibility* for their money decisions. They know their success is up to them, and they own it. Second, millionaires *practice intentionality* with their finances, living on less than they make and exercising discipline in their budgeting. Third, typical millionaires are *goal-oriented.* They think ahead and refuse to be swept away by the current of life. Fourth, and not surprisingly, millionaires are *hard workers.* They do what it takes even when what it takes isn't easy. Fifth and last, we found that millionaires know that wealth building takes *consistency.* They know from experience that wealth building is a long-term game, and they've seen that sticking to the plan over decades leads to millions at retirement. These aren't the character traits *I* think can lead to millions; these are the attributes we *found* in the 10,000 millionaires we studied. As we walk through the next several chapters, I'll give you the cold, hard facts about what these men and women believe compared to the general population. And, when you see these five attributes working in high gear, you'll get a clear picture of what financial independence really looks like—and what it could look like for you.

Over the next five chapters, I'm going to unpack each of these attributes for you. I'll show you not only the characteristics that have led to so many millionaire success stories but also the actions to take to get there yourself. By getting to know these millionaires and applying these attributes and actions to your life, you'll be well on your way to writing your own millionaire story someday.

THE STRANGEST SECRET

Earl Nightingale is a legend to authors, speakers, and radio hosts like me. In 1956, he produced a spoken-word record—the early ancestor of today's audiobook—that became the first spoken-word record to go gold in sales. It sold more than a million copies, which was unheard of for a recording of this type in the fifties. The name of that recording is *The Strangest Secret*, and it has changed countless lives over the past sixty years. What is the "strangest secret"? What is it that makes some succeed where others fail? For Nightingale, it all comes down to one simple truth: we become what we think about. He compares it to planting a seed, saying, "The ground will always return what is planted." Therefore, if you plant tomatoes, you'll get tomatoes. In the same way, if you plant a seed of success in your mind, you'll get success. If you plant a seed of fear and doubt, you'll get a crop of fear and doubt. The ground doesn't *care* what you plant, but it will always *return* what you planted.

Now that we've destroyed the myths about millionaires that hold many people back, I want to challenge you to replace those myths and lies with truth. The truth matters. Every day you are planting seeds in your mind—seeds of hope, wealth, and success or seeds of doubt, fear, and failure. If you want to reap the same harvest that our 10,000 millionaires have reaped, you've got to plant the type of seeds that they've planted. So let's get a better look at the key attributes of the everyday American millionaire. We'll start with something we've already noticed in the stories I've shared, something 97% of millionaires agree on: the power of personal responsibility. You'll see that you—yes, *you*—are responsible for your money, your financial choices, and your dreams of reaching financial independence.

Millionaires Do

- *Believe millionaire status is available to them.*

- *Understand each person starts at a different place and may have more obstacles to overcome, but they don't let obstacles stop them from trying.*

- *Come from all walks of life, all different parts of the country, and all different socioeconomic backgrounds.*

Millionaires Don't ───────────────

- *Buy into the common myths about wealth and the wealthy.*

- *Make excuses or believe their success depends on anyone else.*

- *Let fear and doubt keep them from winning.*

If you live in this great country, there is no reason not to achieve your goals! The only person stopping you is the person in the mirror. Don't let your past be your future. Every day we all have a choice to be productive or wait for others. I prefer to drive my own destiny! Victims need not apply.

—CANDICE, $4 MILLION NET WORTH

Chapter 6

Own It

Millionaires Take Personal Responsibility

We have a crisis of responsibility in this country today. More and more, it seems like we as a society care more about *assigning blame* for our problems than *finding solutions* for our problems. Can't get a job? It's the economy's fault—even if you never went to college and haven't read a book since high school. Can't lose weight? It's the food industry's fault—even if you've never worked out and eat nothing but fast food. Can't get ahead financially? It's the wealthy's fault—even if you've maxed out credit cards and car loans to support your high-end lifestyle. Can't win a game of golf? It's because of the wind. Rear-end another car at a stop light? It's because the other guy hit the brakes too fast. Fail a test? It's because the teacher's out to get you. Does any of this sound familiar?

Ronald Reagan once said, "We must reject the idea that every time a law's broken, society is guilty rather than the lawbreaker. It is time to restore the American precept that each individual is accountable for his actions." That doesn't seem likely in our culture today.

We love holding *others* accountable for our missteps. However, while personal responsibility seems completely MIA in many circles, there's one population where it is not only evident but also dominant: America's everyday millionaires. The men and women we studied have embraced personal responsibility in a way we haven't seen anywhere else, and that sense of responsibility is driving them up to and beyond the millionaire mark.

EVERYDAY MILLIONAIRES

Take Mike and Stephanie, for example. These millionaires from South Carolina are now retired and enjoying the life of their dreams—and they have only themselves to thank for it. Mike came from a middle-class family with two working, well-educated parents. His father was a scientist in the space program, and his mother was a preschool teacher. Because his parents grew up during the Great Depression, they were intentional about teaching Mike the value of hard work, the dangers of debt, and the importance of saving. Mike and his siblings never got an allowance; they had to work for their spending money as children. He even started his own window-washing and shoe-shining businesses at age sixteen. That taught him early on that his finances were up to him and that no one was going to hand him anything he didn't earn for himself.

After completing a PhD in theater, Mike spent his time directing plays and teaching theater classes at a local college. He eventually became a dean of the college of arts and humanities at the school, and later accepted a position as the dean of arts at a school in South Carolina. During this time, he met and married Stephanie, who worked her way through medical school. Throughout their marriage, Mike and Stephanie lived like his parents taught him. They never had a dime of credit card debt, and they maintained a comfortable yet modest lifestyle. Mike said, "It just wasn't important to me to have the best cars or stay at the best hotels." What was important to him? Saving. Mike and Stephanie made saving a priority throughout their marriage—especially when their incomes increased at the top of their careers. When everyone else was spending, they were building wealth. They took advantage of company-sponsored retirement plans and company matches, along with other investments over a long period of time. Even now, in retirement and with a net worth of $2.6 million, they are making smart decisions by holding off on Social Security distributions until age seventy, when they can get the maximum benefit.

Mike and Stephanie attribute their success to their lifelong saving habits, avoiding debt, and working with an investment professional; their commitment to improving themselves; and their earning potential through education. They both knew early on what they wanted their lives to be, and they did whatever it took to make their millionaire dreams a reality. If you want to join them in millionaire status, you need to get a handle on one of the most prevalent character traits we discovered about millionaires: an extreme sense of personal responsibility.

A CRISIS OF RESPONSIBILITY

Most people aren't doing well with their money. Our research team did a study on the state of retirement in America and found that 56% of Americans are losing sleep over their retirement. They aren't sure how they're going to support themselves when they stop working—if they're ever *able* to stop working. Only one in ten are saving the recommended 15% of their income toward retirement. People in or approaching their sixties are starting to freak out, as we found 50% of baby boomers have less than $10,000 saved for retirement. And even the youngest generation of working Americans, the millennials, are feeling the pressure. We found that eight out of ten of them already wished they were investing more toward retirement and wealth building.[22]

That last statistic really stands out to me. Eight in ten say they wish they were investing more. You want to know what I tell people when they say something like that to me? I look them in the eye and say, "Well, why aren't you? If you want to invest more, then invest more. You're the only one who can make that happen." That's when they usually hit me with all the reasons why that's not possible, all the things that make their situation uniquely challenging, and all the excuses they're used to spouting for why they aren't winning yet. Now, I understand that our young people are facing real economic differences from previous generations, but each generation has experienced its own unique challenges. And no matter what challenges we're facing as a society, we still have to be accountable to and for ourselves and work as hard as we can to *overcome* those challenges.

If you struggle with the blame game, let me give it to you straight: Wherever you are financially, it's because you allowed it. Whatever you've accomplished, it's because you did it. Whatever you've failed at, it's because you messed it up. Like Theodore Roosevelt once said, "If you could kick the person in the pants responsible for most of your trouble, you wouldn't sit for a month." If you want to change your circumstances, you've got to change your mind-set about what's really going on here: your money choices, well, they're on you. I know there really are obstacles out there, but I also know millionaire-minded people don't let those obstacles get in their way. Instead, they find a way around—or, better yet, *through*—whatever gets in between them and their goals. Focused, driven, and responsible people find a way to get the job done, and that starts with taking responsibility for solving the problem themselves. Remember, you can do this.

The Buck Stops Here

Our research revealed a huge difference between the typical millionaire and the rest of society when it comes to personal responsibility. As we've already seen, a whopping 97% of millionaires agree with the statement, "I control my own destiny." Let that sink in for a minute. Do you believe that? Do you believe you're in the driver's seat, that you are the one charting your course toward (or away from) success? Or do you think you're being pulled around by other people? When you experience a victory, you want to be able to look at yourself in the mirror, hold your head up high, and say, *I did that*. And when you make a mistake, you need to be able to do the exact same thing. Personal responsibility is about owning your wins and losses and then moving forward with the lessons you learned. Your destiny—good or bad—is in your hands.

And, as we saw in chapter 2, luck has nothing to do with it. The wealthy don't rely on luck; they rely on tried and true methods for building wealth. A surprise bonus at work or an inheritance from an aunt you forgot about is great, but these unexpected windfalls usually won't make or break you financially. Millionaires know it's the daily grind, the step-by-step actions over the long haul that lead to a high net worth. They don't count on anyone else to make them rich, and they don't blame anyone else if they fall short. They focus on things they can control and align their daily habits to the goals they've set for themselves. Then, one day these hardworking men and women cross the millionaire mark—and they only have themselves to thank for it. The bottom line is,

97% of millionaires agree with the statement, "I control my own destiny."

today's millionaires understand that taking personal responsibility for their finances is the first step in getting where they want to be.

MOTIVATION DRIVES RESPONSIBILITY

We've seen that personal responsibility is a key character trait of the wealthy, but what if you aren't naturally prone to taking responsibility for yourself? What if your parents programmed you to blame someone else for all your problems or taught you to look to others to take care of you? Are you doomed to live a sad, victimized, paycheck-to-paycheck life? No. You can change. You get to choose right now to take responsibility for your own life. You can replace the negative thoughts swimming around in your head with new, positive, wealth-building thoughts. That's what millionaires do, as 82% describe themselves as optimists. They're taking control of their thoughts and turning those negative voices into their motivation for change.

Find Your Fuel

Years ago, when I first showed an interest in becoming a speaker and author, a friend pulled me aside. He said something like, "Listen, Hogan, I just don't think you can do it. I don't think you have what it takes to drive a brand, write books, and own a national stage." Now, an experience like that would shut a lot of people down. They'd go home and convince themselves that their friend was right, and they'd never even try to accomplish their big goal. Not me. To be honest, I got mad. *Real* mad. Instead of shutting me down, that experience fired me up. If there was any doubt in my mind before then, it was gone after that conversation. I went home and thought about it for a while. Ultimately, I decided, *He doesn't think I can do it. I'm going to prove him wrong.* And I did. Several years later, a group of us got together to watch a football game at his house, and he pulled me aside. He apologized for what he had said that day, and he admitted that I'd blown past all his expectations. I love this guy, and I had long since forgiven him. However, even though his apology wasn't necessary, I'll admit that it was good to hear.

That experience was one of many times in my life when someone sized me up and tried to tell me no. The problem with that kind of *no* is that it's not really about the circumstances or the opportunities. Instead, that kind of *no* is about *me*. It's not someone saying, "It can't be done"—it's someone saying, "*You* can't do it." There's a huge difference in those two statements. I don't want to sound childish, but when someone tells me I can't do something, it just adds fuel to my fire. It drives me forward and kicks my efforts into an even higher gear. If you want to push me further, just tell me I can't do something. From that point on, it'll be my goal to make you eat those words. I don't just want to prove the other person wrong, though; I want to prove that *I'm* right! That's what I call "looking for the chips." I never want to be weighed down by a chip on my shoulder, so I'm constantly looking for them, taking them off my back, and throwing them in my motivational furnace. I will accept compliments from everyone, but I will accept limitations from *no one*. Instead, I turn those limitations into fuel. And you need to do the same.

As you begin your millionaire journey, you've got to figure out where your motivation comes from. What's driving you forward? What's fueling your wealth-building engine? Maybe you didn't have much growing up, and that old sense of financial stress is driving you. Or maybe your parents were successful, and their success has driven you to pursue your own. Maybe you're starting to get anxious about your retirement or, better yet, starting to *dream* about your retirement. Maybe you have the encouragement of friends and mentors pushing you forward. Your motivation can come from anywhere. Wherever it comes from, though, you've got to harness it and turn it into energy to accomplish your millionaire goals.

Motivated by Our Kids

Millionaires are also motivated by what they learned from their parents and what they hope to pass on to their children. Our study found that 86% of millionaires learned the importance of saving and taking control of their money from their parents. Those parents knew how to save money, too. In fact, 85% of millionaires describe their parents as savers—and of those, 13% said their parents were "extreme savers." That living example made an impact on the next generation, as those savers' children grew up to be millionaires. This clearly shows that parents have the power to fight back against the destructive messages their kids hear from other people and to replace those messages with encouragement and hope. If you want your children to grow up to become millionaires (not counting the millions you may leave them one day), then you need to model millionaire behaviors for them. It's like my friend Rachel Cruze always says, "More is caught than taught." Your kids will learn how to handle money by watching you. Those healthy (or unhealthy) behaviors are passed down from generation to generation. If your parents didn't model healthy millionaire habits for you, you can be the one to turn things around in your family tree. Even if you don't leave your children a pile of money when you die, you *can* leave them the attitudes and attributes that will enable them to reach millionaire status for themselves.

This point was driven home to me as I was writing this. I had received an email from Cindy, a lady I had met several years ago at a speaking engagement in North Carolina. She and her husband, James, had good incomes, but they weren't being intentional about what they were doing. By attending the event I led, they learned the basic principles of wealth building and put those principles to work immediately. They stopped excusing their own financial laziness and took ownership of their finances. As they got their act together, they involved their children and passed down what they were learning about money. Cindy had emailed me to let me know they had hit their goal years earlier than they ever expected. She had just turned in her notice to retire at work—at age forty-five! She wrote, "Chris, you changed our family tree. Our five kids are growing up on a completely different trajectory than where we were headed."

85% of millionaires describe their parents as savers. Of those, **13%** said their parents were "extreme savers."

I wrote back immediately and said, "No, Cindy. *You and James* changed your family tree. I was just the cheerleader!" You see, once this couple stopped buying into all the excuses for why they weren't winning, they turned their entire family's future around. And instead of hiding their mistakes and course corrections from their children, they included the kids in the process. Their passion for giving their kids a great start in life was their motivation to get the job done for themselves. Now, Cindy's retired at forty-five, the family's doing great, and the kids got to watch it happen. It wouldn't surprise me at all if she wrote back in twenty years to let me know all five of her kids were millionaires, too!

KNOW WHERE YOU ARE

By now, I hope you're starting to get a vision for where you want to go financially. You've seen that millionaires are regular people, and the stories from our research should encourage you that you can get to where they are. To do that, though, you've got to know where you are today. Taking responsibility for your millionaire goals begins with taking responsibility for where you are *right now*. That means facing your stuff head-on with no fear, guilt, shame, denial, or excuses. You've got to own it 100%.

Own Your Mess

Ready for some truth? You are ultimately responsible for how well you're doing right now. Wherever you are, however you got there, you've got to own it. It's your responsibility. If your finances are a mess right now, though, that's still good news. Like Dave Ramsey says, "If you're the *problem*, that means you're also the *solution*." Taking ownership of how you got to this point may hurt, but when you do it, you're also taking ownership of the power to turn things around. This is a key characteristic of millionaires. Our study found that 95% of millionaires—almost *all* of them—are willing to quickly admit when they're wrong. They don't lie to themselves or others, and they don't waste time looking for someone to blame. Instead, they own up to their mistakes and start looking for ways to turn things around. That's what personal responsibility is all about. So, if you've driven your finances into a ditch, don't look for someone else to come along and pull you out. It's your problem to fix, and nobody—no charity, boss, or government program—will be more motivated to solve your problems than you are. So let's fix them.

Owning your situation begins with getting a clear picture of where you are—which, when it comes to money, means calculating your net worth. In chapter 1, I explained that net worth is simply everything you *own* minus what you *owe*. It's all your assets minus all your liabilities. That is the barebones, most basic way to track your progress toward millionaire status. Your net worth is essentially the blue dot that shows you exactly where you are on the financial map. You'll never know where you are or how much progress you're making until you start tracking this figure. Calculating this number is just basic math, and it won't take long to do. But don't put it off; do this *right now*. We're starting a journey with this book, and I want you to be able to look back on this day in a few years and know exactly how far you've come. To help, I've put a great net worth calculator on my site, www.chrishogan360.com. Go check it out.

Better Is Available

Once you get a clear picture of your starting point, you'll probably have one of three reactions. I discussed these in detail in my book *Retire Inspired*, but I'll quickly recap them here:

1. *Oh, crap!* This is the realization that you're in pretty bad shape. If your net worth is a negative number, these will probably be the first words out of your mouth.
2. *Oh, boy!* This is the reaction when you see you've got the ball rolling, but you still have a long way to go. This is where you wipe your forehead, dig in, and get back to work.
3. *Oh, yeah!* If you've been diligent about saving and investing for a while, your net worth may make you jump out of your chair and high-five your spouse. This is the realization that you're doing great so far and you're on pace for a sweet finish-line victory.

Most of the people who read this book will have one of the first two reactions when they look at their net worth for the first time—and that's okay. Remember, wealthy people don't lie to themselves or make excuses for screwing things up. They face the truth, admit that they've made some mistakes, own them, and move on. That's what I want you to do right now.

Whatever your net worth reveals, no matter how awesome or how terrible things look today, remember this statement: better is available. Take a deep breath and say that out loud. *Better is available.*

If you're standing in a deep hole, you've got nowhere to go but up. If you're standing at the top of a mountain, you can go climb a higher mountain. You can *always* improve your situation; you just have to stay hungry, take responsibility for where you *are* and where you want to *be*, and be willing to go after it. When you truly believe better is available for you, you're doing two things: First, you're accepting the fact that something better is out there. You're refusing to close yourself off to opportunities and planning long-term. Second, you're making a decision about what you need to do next. It's your responsibility, remember? No one else can do it for you. You're looking at the destination and telling yourself, *That's where I want to go, so I'm going to figure out how to get there.*

Replace Negative Voices with Positive Voices

Of course, once you take responsibility for where you are and set your sights on something better, the world will try to knock you off course. I'm not talking about losing a job or going through a personal tragedy. I'm talking about a friend trying to crush your dreams by making a sarcastic comment about how "people like us" can't become wealthy. You know what I'm talking about. It's like a buddy finding out you're on a diet and immediately offering you a slice of cake. Even if you don't talk openly about your financial goals, you'll be bombarded with messages about how wealth is exclusive and how people like you can't get there. You'll hear all the myths about millionaires that we've already debunked. These things will get stuck in your brain, playing over and over again as you try to make progress. Here's my advice for when those messages play on a loop in your mind: change the tape. Whatever track plays long enough and loud enough in your mind will start to sound like the truth. You can take control of your thoughts and replace false messages with the truth of what we're discovering about millionaires—and the truth that you can become one, too.

In the previous chapter, I shared the wisdom in Earl Nightingale's message *The Strangest Secret*. He taught that we become what we think about, that we are always planting seeds of belief (or doubt) in our minds. If that's true, then we not only need to remove the junk from our brains that's getting in our way, but we also need to replace those false messages with encouragement and truth. For that, you need to be intentional about having a team of positive thinkers in your life.

Our research has shown that we all need to build a network of encouraging, like-minded, and challenging people to support us on our millionaire journey. While almost all the millionaires we studied are self-made, they aren't completely isolated. They are, however, careful about who they allow to speak into their lives. In fact, 98% of them say they actively integrate feedback from other people. Despite their success, they know they always have more to learn, and they look to a supportive network to teach them new things and encourage them along the way.

There are four key relationships you need to incorporate into your life as you work your way up to and beyond the millionaire mark. First, you need a *coach*. This is someone who stands on the sidelines and challenges you to keep making progress. When you fall, this is the voice you hear yelling at you to get up. When you're running the wrong way, this is the one who is screaming to get your attention. This is the person who tells it like is, who won't blow smoke just to make you feel better if you're being stupid. I've had athletic, business, and financial coaches my entire life, and these men and women have played a huge role in the man I've become. Find someone who does the same for you.

Second, you need a *mentor*. Our study revealed that 86% of millionaires actively get advice from mentors. This is someone who has done what you want to do. They're on the same journey, but they're a few miles ahead of you. They've seen the dangers and overcome the obstacles you haven't reached yet, and they're happy to share what they've learned. Of course, books and seminars are great ways to learn, but nothing beats a wise mentor taking you by the hand and showing you how to do what they've already accomplished for themselves. And no, I'm not talking about a boring, forced, semi-uncomfortable weekly breakfast meeting. If that works for you, great. But I personally prefer to keep things more casual. The mentors who have meant the most to me are the ones who seem to pop in on my life every now and then, dropping wisdom in the moment. Don't overthink your mentor strategy. Just be on the lookout for someone who can speak into your life and take them out for coffee once every few months. Save up some questions over time so you can have a deep, meaningful conversation when you meet. Ask them their stories, learn what makes them tick. Ask them to tell you their biggest failures and what they learned from them. Keep things informal and learn as much as you can.

Third, you need a *cheerleader*. This is someone who believes in you and is there to encourage you no matter what. All the years I spent on the football field made me realize the value of having cheering fans on the sidelines. Sure, I had coaches yelling at me, giving me instructions, calling plays, and trying to keep my head in the game, but sometimes I didn't need marching orders; I just needed encouragement. I needed someone to call out my name, smile, and cheer me on. For people trying to become a millionaire, the best cheerleaders are millionaires who have already crossed that line themselves. They know the challenges you're up against, and they'll be a constant reminder that you can make it. That's something even our closest friends sometimes can't do, especially if they don't think your millionaire aspirations are possible.

Fourth, you need a *friend*. This one is simple, but it is so powerful. Sure, you need to focus on your goals and aim your efforts in that direction, but you don't want to spend every waking minute thinking about, dreaming about, or worrying about your millionaire journey. You need to have some fun! Friends remind us that life is about more than building wealth. And, especially true for old friends, they remind us who we are and where we've come from. True friends care about us as individuals. They help keep us rooted so we don't lose sight of who we really are. Don't underestimate the quality-of-life value in that. You never want to build wealth at the cost of your relationships.

PLOT YOUR COURSE

One of the most interesting speaking gigs I've ever had was with an elite group of military servicemembers. When our time was done, I felt like I had learned more from them than they had from me. After a session, I was talking to some of them about military preparation. I asked them how they're able to adapt so quickly when something goes wrong. They said something like, "Actually, things never really go 'wrong,' because we plan for and train for everything. If something happens that derails one plan, we just move on to the next."

For example, they told me about an incident they had on a mission in enemy waters. One of their boats became disabled, so the guys in the second boat immediately jumped into action. They threw all their unnecessary gear into the water to make room for the other men. They went from two boats loaded with men and gear to one boat carrying twice as many people and half as much stuff in a matter of seconds. And, of course, they knew exactly what pieces of gear they could toss overboard without endangering the mission. My day can feel ruined if I have to stop to change a flat tire, but these guys made crucial decisions, consolidated their resources, and got on with the mission in less than a minute without missing a beat. But like they told me, this is something they had trained for. They explained that, when you plan for the obstacles, they don't shake your confidence or interrupt your progress when they happen. I left that speaking engagement with a new attitude about wealth building taken straight out of the Special Forces playbook: *I am going to win—no matter what.* To ensure that victory, though, I must make a plan and stick to it.

Set Your Destination

When you program your GPS, you need to know two things: where you are and where you're going. You should have already identified your starting point earlier in this chapter by calculating your net worth. Now, it's time to get a picture of where you want to go. If you're married, you and your spouse need to have what I call a "dream meeting," in which you work together to paint a crystal-clear picture of your retirement vision. If you're single, you're not off the hook; you just need to paint the picture for yourself. I want you to envision every part of your retirement lifestyle—where you want to live, where and how often you want to travel, what car you want to drive, what kind of health care you want to be able to afford, and how much money you need each month to support your dream retirement lifestyle. Account for all of it, and don't let any negative voices hold you back. Remember, this is a *dream* meeting, so don't be scared to dream.

Once you have that retirement vision clear in your head, it's time to figure out how much money you'll need to accomplish as much of that dream as possible. To clear away any guesses and speculation, I've developed a tool that will make these calculations drop-dead simple. I call it the R:IQ, which stands for *Retire Inspired Quotient*. You can use this tool for free on my website, www.chrishogan360.com. When you're done, you'll know exactly how much money you'll need in your nest egg to support the life you want *and* how much you need to save each month between now and then to make that happen. We take all the guesswork out of it. Once you have your retirement vision locked and loaded, head over to my site to take the R:IQ.

Get Help

Next, you need to plan for how to hit the numbers you set for yourself in the R:IQ tool. Unless you're a professional investment advisor, I strongly encourage you to get some help with this step. The theme of this chapter is personal responsibility, but that doesn't mean you have to do all this alone. Like I said previously, you're solely responsible for the outcome, but you can get as much help as you want to reach your goals. That's what millionaires do. We found that 68% of millionaires used an investment professional to achieve their high net worth. Remember, these are regular people with regular jobs, not investing geniuses. Even though they took ownership of their actions and outcomes, they didn't shy away from getting help and counsel when needed.

EVERYDAY MILLIONAIRES

Take Michael and Valerie, a millionaire couple from Philadelphia, for example. They both worked in the human resource field for thirty years before retiring. They came from middle-class backgrounds and admit that their families had *enough*, but neither family was particularly skilled at handling money. Michael and Valerie set out to learn how to handle money for themselves, and their efforts paid off. Like most millionaires we've highlighted, this couple lived modestly and saved like crazy. They didn't drive fancy, brand-new cars, live in big houses, or take expensive vacations. Instead, Michael says their saving habits were the most important factor in becoming millionaires. They maxed out their 401(k) contributions, and they even deferred their financial bonuses at work into a special savings account.

Over time, this aggressive saving paid off, and they began to build real wealth. At that point, the couple enlisted the help of an investment professional to help them reach their financial goals. This person became a trusted mentor to the couple over the years and was instrumental in their wealth building. Today, Michael and Valerie are retired with a net worth of nearly $3 million, and they are still with the same investment professional more than twenty years later. They have discovered the power of a long-term, trusted investment professional as part of their wealth-building team, and they see no reason to break those ties now that they're living their retirement dream.

If you need help finding an investing pro in your area, visit www.chrishogan360.com and try SmartVestor, a program that connects you with financial professionals who can put together a plan for your wealth-building goals. This is someone who can guide you on your millionaire journey and help you identify risks and opportunities. Getting the help of a professional may seem intimidating, but don't let intimidation stop you from reaching your goals. Millionaire-minded people don't let the unknown scare them off. Instead, 94% of the millionaires we studied say they're willing to try difficult things to get new results. They know that a little change and challenge are necessary at times. Getting some guidance from a financial pro may seem difficult now, but the rewards are worth it!

You'll want to meet with your investing professional once or twice a year to review your investments, discuss new risks and goals, and make sure your investing plan is still taking you where you want to go. Too many people take a "set it and forget it" approach to their investments, but that leaves too much potential money on the table. Stay plugged into your investments and let your investing pro mentor you on how to play the game. Remember, your wealth building is a long-term play, so settle in with someone you're comfortable with and enjoy the ride.

IF IT'S TO BE, IT'S UP TO ME

I was blessed with a great mother who poured into me. She never let me overlook opportunities, and she always stressed how much potential I had in school, sports, and business. She was also a huge proponent of personal responsibility. She taught me from an early age that I was ultimately responsible for my wins and losses. One of her favorite sayings was, "If it's to be, it's up to me." I heard that at least once a week growing up. It was her fallback statement whenever my brother or I felt like whining about whatever trouble we were facing at the time. She didn't have time for our little pity parties, and she didn't want us to make time for them, either.

When I was in high school, Mama Hogan made a cross-stitch of that quote and encouraged me to keep it with me throughout high school, college, and into my adult life. It was her little reminder that, wherever I was and whatever I was doing, no one was going to hand me anything. If I wanted to accomplish something, it was my responsibility to make it happen. Sitting in our little Kentucky home, she'd say, "Chris, you're bigger than this town." Now, there is absolutely nothing wrong with my hometown; it's a great place to live with great people. But my mother was teaching me to think bigger. She wanted me to believe that I could go anywhere and do anything I put my mind to. She believed in me and in my ability to become successful, and she made me believe that for myself. My mom filled me with these messages throughout my entire life, so that's the mind-set I have now toward every goal I want to accomplish.

As I'm typing this in my home office right now, the little framed cross-stitch she made thirty years ago is prominently displayed on the bookshelf right beside me. It's a constant reminder of the millionaire mind-set of a single mom in middle-class Kentucky. *If it's to be, it's up to me.* It's a lesson I learned early on and one I still believe to this day. And, more importantly, it's a characteristic of every millionaire I've ever met. If you want to bust through the $1 million barrier, you've got to accept the fact that you're the only one who can make it happen. No one is going to break down your door and force $1 million into your hands. It's up to you to own it, to get out there, and do it for yourself.

Millionaires Do

- **Own their mistakes and change course when needed.** *95% of millionaires are willing to quickly admit when they're wrong.*

- **Take advice from others.** *98% of millionaires say they actively integrate feedback from other people, and 86% actively seek advice from mentors.*

- **Use financial planners.** *68% of millionaires have used a financial planner to achieve their high net worth.*

Millionaires Don't

- **Think negatively.** *82% of millionaires describe themselves as optimists.*

- **Let the unknown scare them off.** *94% of millionaires say they're willing to try difficult things to get new results.*

I don't identify with "rich." I've seen rich and we're not that, but we don't sweat over an unexpected expense, and we enjoy an occasional splurge on ourselves. Yet we still use coupons. Our kids think we're living paycheck to paycheck because we live that way. They also think we're much poorer than their friends. We use that as a teaching moment, constantly trying to spin their understanding of a culture of consumerism.

—JUDY, $2.7 MILLION NET WORTH

Chapter 7

Live on Less
Than You Make

Millionaires Practice Intentionality

In 1991, my college football team won a national championship. We had worked hard and played hard all season, and we became the first team in the school's history to win a national title. We were pumped. All the blood, sweat, and tears we left on the field all year had paid off, and those teammates had become like brothers to me. To commemorate the incredible year we'd had, all the guys decided to get a team tattoo on their legs—a constant reminder of what we had achieved together. I wanted that tiger paw tattoo more than almost anything, but I couldn't do it. As the guys left for the tattoo parlor, I could hear some of them saying, "Hey! Hogan's not coming!" I don't think I've ever felt more left out in my life.

So, why didn't I go? Well, I mentioned earlier that I planned on becoming an FBI agent. That meant, even as a college student, I had to be intentional about the decisions I made. I couldn't get a victory tattoo because I couldn't get any permanent distinguishing marks on my body. That tiger paw, cool as it was, could have gotten me killed in the line of duty! As much as I wanted to join my brothers in celebrating our victory, I had another goal in mind—a long-term goal that directed many of the decisions I made as a young man. I knew, if I really wanted to be an agent, I had to be intentional about how I acted, my grades, where I went to school, and the people I hung out with. The picture of myself as an FBI agent became the lens through which I viewed different choices and opportunities. If I had the chance to do something that put my career goal in jeopardy, I said no. Being aware of what I wanted in life gave me the clarity and perspective I needed to stay on track and make wise choices. I didn't know it at the time, but I was practicing one of the key millionaire attributes: intense intentionality.

WHAT IS INTENTIONALITY?

In the previous chapter, we saw that millionaires take full responsibility for their lives—good or bad. Now we're going to focus on another millionaire mind-set that goes hand in hand with personal responsibility, and that's the quality of being intentional. You see, nobody *accidentally* ends up retiring with millions in the bank, just like no football team *accidentally* wins "The Big Game." Those victories come from a ton of hard work and thousands of daily decisions. And, as we studied over 10,000 millionaires, we noticed a pattern of intense intentionality that dominated their lives. We saw that they viewed their lives through a lens—just like I did when I had FBI aspirations—and they measured every decision through that lens. I'll share several of those findings throughout this chapter as we get a clear picture of the typical *intentional* millionaire.

Deciding vs. Sliding

I like to describe intentionality in terms of *deciding* versus *sliding*. When you decide to do something, you're in control. You're making a conscious choice about what you want to do, and you're taking the time to measure the pros and cons. You may not get it right every time, but you're being intentional about what you do with your life. You're *happening to things* instead of letting other things *happen to you*. Instead of drifting through life, you're hopping in the driver's seat with your GPS locked on your destination.

Compare that to what I call *sliding*. When you slide into a decision, you're being a passive passenger in your own life. You're just going with the flow, drifting wherever the current takes you. You aren't in control of anything, you aren't directed toward anything, and you have no idea where you'll end up. I don't know anyone who would outright say that's what they want for their lives, and yet that's exactly how they're living. They let life knock them around for forty years, and then they're surprised when they hit retirement flat broke. In contrast, the millionaires we studied weren't surprised by where they ended up. They arrived at the destinations they had worked toward their whole lives. And they did it one decision at a time. Frank and Alice are a great example of this.

EVERYDAY MILLIONAIRES

Frank and Alice—a millionaire couple from New York—understood the difference between deciding versus sliding. As a boy, Frank lived with his parents and grandparents, who were German immigrants. He remembers his father and grandfather not only as hard workers but also as frugal spenders. His grandfather especially hated debt in all forms, and his warnings against the dangers of debt and living beyond your means still ring in Frank's ears half a century later. When he graduated high school, he skipped college and went to work on Wall Street. He went on to hold several different types of jobs in the financial industry, teaching himself the ins and outs of investments and wealth building along the way.

No matter how sophisticated some of the things he saw on Wall Street appeared, though, Frank never moved too far beyond his grandfather's simple way of life. He and Alice spent their entire working lives saving, investing, avoiding debt, and sticking to their plan, which led them to a net worth of $6 million. When we asked why they thought there weren't more millionaires in the country today, they said most people are more concerned with keeping up with the Joneses than they are about leaving a legacy for their own children. As for intentionality, Frank says, "Too many people focus on *now* instead of thinking about *later*. But, if you don't think about and plan for the future, you won't have any money for retirement."

Frank touched on something that came up in many of our millionaire interviews: spending versus saving. First, we found that 94% of millionaires say they live on less than they make—compared to 55% of the general population. Second, 95% of millionaires say they plan ahead and save in advance for big expenses—compared to 67% of the general population. Millionaire-minded people like Frank and Alice have a picture in their heads of where they want to be financially, and they know that *sliding* behaviors, like thoughtless spending and credit card living, won't get them there.

Instead, they choose to *decide* their way into wealth, and that usually comes down to living on the plans they make for themselves. That's why 93% of the millionaires we studied say they stick to the budgets they create, compared to 77% of the general population. Millionaires know that building and maintaining wealth come down to how well they manage their money—and sticking to a budget is the most basic way to do that. Sure, if you've got $2 million in the bank, it'd be easy to excuse busting the budget on a big, unplanned purchase, but that's not what the typical millionaire does. They decide beforehand how they want to spend their money, and they stick to the plan.

We found other examples of the millionaire *deciding* versus *sliding* mentality in how they choose to spend their money. Contrary to what you may see on TV, the average millionaire lives a modest life without many extravagances. For example, the typical millionaire spends $200 or less per month on restaurants. I wish I had known this twenty years ago. When I first started to take control of my money, I was shocked to discover how much money I'd been wasting on restaurants every month. Talk about *sliding*. It ticks me off to think of all the money I let slip

95% of millionaires plan ahead and save up for big expenses, compared to **67%** of the general population.

through my fingers because of careless, thoughtless restaurant spending. Millionaires don't do that; they put a modest restaurant budget down on paper, and then they stick to it. They aren't that concerned with what anyone else thinks, either. Only 7% of the millionaires we studied felt pressure to keep up with their friends and families when it came to spending. The rest were content with their older cars, modest homes, and average $35 pair of *jeans*. That's right, we asked 10,000 millionaires how much they spent on jeans. I told you before that we wanted to know everything about these folks.

LIVE ON LESS THAN YOU MAKE

More than half (51%) of the millionaires in our study believe the top factor holding people back from becoming millionaires is a basic lack of financial discipline. These wealthy men and women demonstrate their discipline with habits you wouldn't normally attribute to millionaires. We've already seen that 94% of millionaires live on less than they make, and 95% plan ahead and save up for big purchases. That planning takes different forms, but most of them (64%) still live on a budget, even though they are financially independent. And, believe it or not, 93% of millionaires use coupons all or some of the time while shopping. That means there's a good chance the crazy coupon lady holding you up in the grocery store line is a millionaire! Speaking of shopping, 85% of millionaires still use a shopping list when buying groceries—even though they could afford to buy anything they want in the store. Millionaires also make a habit of actually *paying* for what they purchase. We found that 96% of millionaires never carry a balance on a credit card. So let's break it down: millionaires live on less than they make, save for big purchases, and spend wisely. Or, to make it crystal clear, they live on a budget and stay out of debt. It's not rocket science.

93% of millionaires use coupons when shopping.

Budgeting for Abundance

As a regular guest on several national TV news programs, I am often on panels with other financial experts. Not surprisingly, I disagree with my fellow "experts" more often than not. However, I was listening to a rental real estate podcast recently and almost spit coffee out of my mouth when I heard something especially dumb. They were talking about building wealth through real estate, and then they went off on a rant about how self-defeating the act of budgeting is. They said a budget represents a scarcity mentality—where you're trying to maximize every nickel and dime—while an abundance mentality gives you freedom *from* a budget. Your goal, they suggested, should be to build enough wealth and cash flow that you don't have to put the "restriction" of a budget on yourself. There's just no other way for me to say it: That's crazy. That's the kind of ignorant, uninformed, and dangerous advice that leads people into careless spending and clueless money mismanagement. I've seen it over and over in my time as a financial coach. And that's not how real millionaires behave.

Millionaires don't *accidentally* live on less than they make. They do it on purpose because they have a plan. They're *deciding*. Living without a budget, though, is the very definition of sliding into misfortune. It represents spending your hard-earned money with no real plan in place. Your budget is your financial road map. It shows you all the twists and turns that are coming up each month. If you're going through the month without a plan, you're driving without a map and hoping to end up in the land of millions. Take it from me and the 10,000 people we studied: that's not going to happen.

A budget helps you identify what I call "money leaks." Those are all the little holes and cracks in your spending habits that let your money leak out of your wallet—without you even realizing what's going on. You know what I'm talking about. How many times have you gotten to the end of the month without a dime to your name and with no idea where your whole paycheck went? A few extra groceries here, a couple of restaurant meals there, a few stops at Starbucks every week, and then *BOOM*. You're broke. I've seen this happen with high-income, two-income couples, and I've seen it happen with minimum-wage single parents. Even though this looks and feels like a *money* problem, most of the time it's not. Instead, it's a *behavior* problem—one you have the power to change. No matter what kind of income you have, if you stay disciplined and make a plan for where your money is going, you'll find your pockets full long after payday.

Budget with Intentionality

Just to make sure we're all on the same page, let me clarify what a budget is. It's simply a spending plan, a way to track all the money coming in and all the money going out in a month. It can be as simple as a sheet of paper or as complex as a multipage spreadsheet. Or you could use an online budgeting tool and mobile app to create and track your spending. There are several of those available, but my personal favorite is EveryDollar at www.everydollar.com. Whatever format you use, the goal is the same. You want to plan for the month ahead by writing down everything you need to spend money on and making sure your monthly income will cover it all. This is how you can emulate the millionaire behavior of living on less than you make. If you don't know how much you have coming in and how much you have going out, you'll never know if you're overspending—especially if you're spending blind by using a credit card.

While creating a monthly budget is absolutely vital, your work isn't done once you've got the plan on the page. The next step is just as important: you have to stick to the plan. Again, that's what millionaires do. Remember, 93% of millionaires stick to the budgets they create, compared to 77% of the general population. These people take the time to make a plan, but then they throw it out the window with impulse purchases and lazy spending. Why even bother? That's like programming your GPS when you get in the car and then throwing it in the back seat when you put the car in drive. It just doesn't make sense. Because of their dedication to sticking to the budgets they make, almost none of the millionaires we studied

(96%) have ever had a past-due bill. They pay their bills on time because they know when they're due and how much they are, and they've accounted for that on their spending plan. The budget gives them built-in accountability and keeps them on track.

Also, don't miss the fact that these millionaires stick to their budgets *even though they can afford anything they want.* I didn't say 93% used to stick to their budgets; I said they still do! That means you never outgrow the need for a budget, even after you become a millionaire. In fact, I'd argue that the more money you have, the greater your responsibility is to manage it well. Losing $1,000 due to sloppy spending is bad enough; I don't even want to think about losing $100,000 just because I was too lazy to manage it.

Redeeming the Word Budget

I've found that many people hate the word *budget.* It can carry a lot of bad emotional connotations or bring up painful memories of old family drama. It can also sound restrictive or feel like a financial cage. I wonder if that's why the hosts of the rental real estate podcast episode I listened to hated the idea of a budget. If you're coming to the table already predisposed against creating a budget, let me help you reframe the whole idea. First of all, a budget is not a financial straitjacket, and it's not surrendering all your control. Instead, a budget is a tool that will give you more control over your money than you've ever had. It enables you to make your money work harder and go further than you can imagine. If you don't believe me, then believe the 10,000 millionaires we studied—most of whom built their wealth by living on and sticking to a budget. I don't think all those thousands of millionaires feel caged in by a budget they can't control. Rather, based on the overwhelming number of millionaires who stick to their budgets even after hitting millionaire status, I imagine they see the budget as the tool they used to exercise complete control over their money.

Second, a budget eliminates all the confusion and mystery around where your money goes each month and replaces it with a hyper-awareness of how hard your money is working for you. It makes the financial "slide" impossible because you're tracking every dollar. The first time we created a monthly budget, we realized we'd been spending almost $1,200 a month on groceries. I had no idea we were wasting so much money on garbage we didn't need. As we settled into our monthly budget, we kept "finding" new money because we had cut off the financial slide for good.

Third, a budget puts your money to work. If you want to become a millionaire, you must be intensely intentional about every dollar you have coming in and going out. A budget makes that intentionality easy. As you get started, I want to suggest three priorities to get the biggest bang out of your budget. These should be the first things you spend money on each month. First, you need to practice generous giving. I'll talk more about the power of giving and its relation to wealth building later in this book, but for now, put giving at the top of your budget and start experimenting with it. Second, make sure you are planning for your saving and investing. Too often we pay ourselves last, meaning we pay all the bills *and* *then* save and invest anything that's left. The problem is, when you put saving last, you probably won't have any money left to save after you plan for everything else. Don't be ashamed to make yourself a priority. Third, if you have any type of debt except a mortgage, you need to squeeze every dollar you can out of your budget to pay that debt off as quickly as possible. Debt, as we'll see below, will kill your millionaire aspirations. Wealthy people don't waste time and money on debt, and neither should you.

Budgeting Requires Teamwork (If You're Married)

If you're married, your budget must be a team effort. Too often in my coaching career, I've seen one spouse try to control the finances while dragging their partner along for the ride. I've also seen plenty of disinterested spouses surrender control of the family finances to their nerdier better half, but that's a bad plan too. What happens if the nerd in the relationship dies unexpectedly? Losing a spouse is tragic enough on its own, but you don't want it to completely wreck your family's financial progress too. When you work together on the budget, you're working together on your dreams. Ideally, you'll both achieve your goals together, but if you don't, you want to make sure your spouse and kids will be able to enjoy what you've worked for even if you're not there to enjoy it with them.

When I coach couples on how to start the budgeting process, I always suggest they have one big budget meeting every month. In that meeting, they work together to plan out their spending for the month ahead. They account for every penny of their income (both incomes if they both work), and they write down every penny they'll need to spend. Then, when they are sure they have the budget just right, they agree to act like millionaires and *stick to the plan*. As they get used to living on a budget, I also suggest they have weekly mini-meetings to check in on how it's going. No budget is perfect, and minor adjustments should be expected throughout the month—especially if budgeting is a new practice. So I recommend weekly touchpoints so the couple has a dedicated time to review the spending a week at a time, make any adjustments that are necessary, and hold each other accountable to the budget commitment they made to each other. On that note, let me introduce you to Ted and Diane, one millionaire couple who are a perfect picture of financial teamwork.

EVERYDAY MILLIONAIRES

Ted and Diane admit they were completely broke when they got married. They each brought a pile of student-loan debt into the marriage, and neither had a strong financial background. However, they had something that made all the difference in the world: each other. From the start of their married life, they sat down at the kitchen table with a basic paper budget, doing their best to live on less than they made and attack their debt. "Our starting salaries . . . weren't great," Ted said, "but we thought it was more money than we'd ever seen." After years of living as broke college and grad students, they didn't let their new incomes go to their heads. Instead, they were intentional about maximizing every dollar. First, they saved up an emergency fund—something they maintain to this day. Then, they declared war on their student loans, throwing every dollar they could at them. They decided to delay the purchase of their first home until the loans were paid off because they didn't want any distractions. "We avoided 'stuffitis' [and] practiced delayed gratification," they said. When the student loans were paid off, the couple purchased a home and started investing 15% of their income into retirement accounts. They worked together every step of the way, and neither ran ahead of the other. They wanted to win as a team—and they did.

Today, Ted and Diane are in their mid-forties. They just recently paid off their fifteen-year mortgage on their $300,000 home, they have college savings accounts for their kids' upcoming college expenses, and they have more than $1 million in retirement accounts. With all those things taken care of, and with at least twenty years to go before retirement, Ted and Diane are sitting pretty. Ted said, "We have piled up our plunder, and now we are going to live a life full of options while maintaining our commitment to giving to the church and others." The budget was the cornerstone of Ted and Diane's financial plan from day one, and that hasn't changed now that they've hit the millionaire mark—and they say it never will.

There are a million other things I could say about budgeting, but I'll leave those to other books and authors. If budgeting is new to you, though, I strongly suggest two things. First, pick up a copy of Dave Ramsey's *The Total Money Makeover*. It's the best book out there on taking control of your money and getting on a plan to beat debt. Second, check out the free budgeting tool called EveryDollar. The website and mobile apps are great, and it's an easy way to build and track a budget with just a few clicks.

Millionaires Stay Away from Debt

I want to be as clear as I can here: the average millionaire stays away from debt. As we saw earlier, 96% of millionaires never carry a credit card balance and 95% plan ahead and save up for big purchases. I can hear the excuses now. "But, Chris, of course they don't *need* to use debt. They're millionaires now!" If that's what you're thinking, you aren't hearing me. I don't just mean these men and women don't use debt *now*; I mean they have lived their whole lives by these basic principles. In fact, nearly three-quarters of the millionaires we studied have never carried a credit card balance in their lives! Millionaires know what most people in our society don't: debt will hold you back and prevent you from reaching your financial goals.

I'm not just talking about credit card debt, either. Let's look at the driving habits of most millionaires for a minute. Do you think the typical millionaire drives a shiny new Lexus or Mercedes? Not likely. Do you think the typical millionaire wakes up on Saturday morning, decides to buy a new car by lunch, and drives a brand-new SUV home by dinner? The stats say no. When I say 95% save up for big purchases, that includes cars.

73% of millionaires have never carried a credit-card balance in their lives.

Rather than hitting the lot and buying a brand-new car, we found the average millionaire drives a four-year-old car with 41,000 miles on it. And eight out of ten millionaire car buyers drive it away debt-free without carrying a car payment behind them. These wealthy people know that car payments and loan interest won't move them forward to financial independence.

If you've never calculated what a lifetime of car payments is really costing you, this will blow your mind. Cars.com reports that the average new-car payment is $509 a month.[23] If you did what millionaires do and paid cash for slightly used cars instead, you'd have $509 a month to invest toward retirement and wealth building. In thirty years, that $509 per month investment would break the millionaire mark at $1.1 million. In thirty-five years, it would hit $1.82 million. And—this is crazy—that same $509 per month investment would be worth $2.97 million in forty years. So, if you're in your thirties or forties right now, I just showed you how to become a multimillionaire with one simple trick. Like I've been saying, *anyone* can become a millionaire in America—even if you only invest the average car payment.

Debt is a mind-set that will wreck your wealth-building goals no matter where you are financially. If you genuinely want to become a millionaire someday, then you need to start acting like a millionaire *today*. That means taking control of your money, making a plan for your spending, and staying far away from debt in all its forms. Sure, that's countercultural advice, but we want to be millionaires, remember?

If It Ain't Broke, Don't Fix It

Budgeting and staying out of debt aren't only used to *achieve* financial independence; they're the same habits millionaires use to *maintain* it. Maggie and her husband, Tom, are great examples of this kind of long-term intentional living. This millionaire couple spends part of the year in Colorado and part of the year in Florida. Sounds nice, right? But Maggie would be the first one to tell you this here-and-there living situation didn't happen accidentally. It took decades of planning and sacrifice to make their long-term goal a reality. Here's their story:

EVERYDAY MILLIONAIRES

Maggie was raised on a farm in rural Illinois in what she calls a financially conservative, frugal household. The family never had much when she was young, and Maggie didn't even have indoor plumbing until she was nine. Her mother sewed clothes for Maggie and her siblings, and the family grew their own vegetables and raised livestock for food. Restaurants were a luxury they almost never experienced. In fact, Maggie's first restaurant meal was at age eleven—and she paid for it herself with money she had saved.

Maggie met and married Tom while in college, and the Colorado couple shared a millionaire dream from the start of their relationship. Neither came from wealth, but they dreamed of one day passing the millionaire mark and having a vacation home. They kept that goal in mind for decades, and it was always a part of every big financial discussion they ever had. They sacrificed a lot of luxuries to make that dream a reality, and they used intentional decisions to take them closer to their goal. While working, the couple lived only on Tom's salary and saved Maggie's salary from her job as a dietician in the public school system. Maggie is a master couponer and says she never pays full price for anything. They only go out to eat once a week (if that). They make their own coffee instead of visiting coffee shops and stick to a shopping list whenever they're at the grocery store. They're always vigilant against impulse purchases and unnecessary spending.

By keeping their goal in mind and being intentional about their financial decisions, Maggie and Tom hit their retirement goals in their fifties and topped it off by buying a vacation home in Florida, where they spend part of the year. When we asked Maggie what her advice was to someone who wants to do what they did, she simply said, "Decide what's important to you and stick to it." This couple, worth $2 million, knew early on that their decisions had the power to take them closer to their dream or further away from it. They chose to *decide* their way into wealth, just like all the other millionaires we studied. Then, even though they had plenty of money, they maintained their wealth by doing the same simple, intentional things that got them there.

CHOOSING INTENTIONALITY

Intentionality comes down to two things: sacrifice and choices. You have to know what you're willing to let go of. If I haven't been clear in this chapter, let me break it down for you. You've got to let go of the stupid things that are stealing your potential—things like debt, inattention, and wandering aimlessly through life. Instead, you've got to take on millionaire behaviors—like living on less than you make, budgeting, and making active, intentional decisions about who you want to be and how you want to live. Being intentional gives you options. It opens the door to more choices than ever before, but it also demands some sacrifices—and some of those sacrifices will hurt.

If you've been walking around with your head in a fog, unplugged from the day-to-day reality of your life, then I've got a three-part plan that will wake you up and shake you out of your unmotivated stupor. I call it the Triple A Process for Improvement: assess, acknowledge, and activate:

1. *Assess your current situation.* Be honest about where you spend your time, money, and attention. Ask yourself if those investments are paying off for you. Are they taking you closer to or further from your goals? Don't lie to yourself. Remember, millionaires are honest with themselves, even when faced with their own failure.
2. *Acknowledge what kind of life you want to have.* This is where your high-definition millionaire dream comes into play. Imagine exactly the life you want to have—and hang on to that picture.
3. *Activate your plan to get there.* Intentionality demands activation. Nobody ever crossed the $1 million mark by sitting on the sofa watching TV for forty hours per week. That's how you slide further and further away from your goals.

So, what are you going to do? Are you going to settle for the slide, or are you bold enough to *decide* your way into wealth? The choice is yours, but you need to choose right now. You have to decide if you want to live out of control or if you want to be the CFO of your household by living on less than you make, budgeting, and avoiding debt. We've seen that a life of intentionality requires a lot of choices—and this is the first one. You can do this. It's up to you. Don't blow it.

Millionaires Do

- **Live on less than they make.** 94% of millionaires say they live on less than they make, compared to 55% of the general population.

- **Plan ahead and pay cash.** 95% of millionaires save up for big expenses, compared to 67% of the general population.

- **Use coupons.** 93% of millionaires use coupons when shopping.

- **Use shopping lists and stick to them.** 85% of millionaires still use a shopping list when buying groceries.

- **Drive older cars with no car payments.** The average millionaire drives a four-year-old car with 41,000 miles on it, and 82% of millionaires have no car payments.

Millionaires Don't

- **Go out to eat every night.** *The typical millionaire spends $200 or less per month on restaurants.*

- **Try to impress anyone.** *Only 7% of millionaires feel pressure to keep up with their friends and families when it comes to spending.*

- **Pay their bills late.** *96% of millionaires have never had a past-due bill.*

- **Have credit card debt.** *73% of millionaires have never carried a credit card balance in their lives.*

We lived in the same $125,000 house we bought in year five of our marriage—even after we retired at age forty-seven. Our coworkers kept moving up in house, but we didn't like giving up the almost 10% transaction cost to sell and move. We figure we saved about half a house by not keeping up with our peer group. We bought a $600,000 house for my wife's parents (with cash) and eventually moved into the house when they passed away.

—BILL AND LYNDA, $9.5 MILLION NET WORTH

Chapter 8

Think Ahead

Millionaires Are Goal-Oriented

One of my favorite stories from our research is about Catherine, a millionaire from Seattle. She understood the power of setting goals for herself—goals that would stretch her beyond her comfort zone and would be the fuel to make her dreams a reality. Here's her story:

EVERYDAY MILLIONAIRE ─────────────────────

Catherine grew up in a single-parent household after her mom passed away when she was young. As a little girl, Catherine idolized her dad and wanted to be just like him—a pilot. Even though women weren't commonly accepted as pilots at the time, Catherine set that goal for herself and never let it go. After college, she went to work in the airline industry but, because female pilots were unheard of, Catherine spent five years as a flight attendant while she honed her piloting skills. By age twenty-six, she started working as a pilot for a small regional airline. She continued to break down the barriers in her way and was hired to fly for a large commercial airline at age thirty. From a young age, Catherine never lost sight of her piloting dreams. She just kept hammering away at them until the world caught up to her.

Her goals weren't restricted to flying, either. As she began to earn greater income, Catherine set her sights on financial independence. She started reading books on real estate and even took a class to learn about investments. Her education turned into concrete financial goals, and she began investing regularly into mutual funds. She kept her eye on the prize over the years as she continued to advance in her career, weighing all her financial decisions against her millionaire goals. She cut back on her restaurant budget to free up more money to invest. She even stopped buying coffee when she wasn't flying because she could drink as much coffee as she wanted for free on the plane. She was committed to putting every dollar to work for her millionaire goals, because she was determined to keep the millionaire promise she had made to herself.

Today, of course, Catherine has reached her goal of financial independence with a whopping $3.4 million net worth! With those goals met, she's already looking to the future again and setting concrete goals for what she wants her wealth to do after she's gone. Not only will she leave money to her loved ones, but she'll also leave a nice scholarship fund for students who want to learn to fly. Even when she's gone, Catherine's knack for setting and crushing goals will be a blessing to her family, friends, and a whole new generation of pilots.

Do you think Catherine believed this was possible when she was twenty-one years old and couldn't find work as a pilot? I do. I think she had a crystal-clear image of her future—even when the odds seemed stacked against her—and she had the heart and determination to make it a reality. That's what millionaires do: they set goals. They *have* to, because becoming a millionaire takes a long time for most people. Remember, real millionaires don't bother trying to get rich quick; they strive to build wealth over many years. If that's your plan, too, then you need to set financial goals for yourself. Let's take a look at how to do that and what those goals should be.

MILLIONAIRES ARE PLANNERS

Our research found that 92% of millionaires developed a long-term plan for their money, compared to 60% of the general population. That means these men and women are always thinking ahead—not just to next week or next month, but well into the next decade. They know what they want to accomplish, and they're putting their money to work to make it happen. Their plan helps them avoid distractions and the "shiny object syndrome" that the general population suffers from, because millionaires aren't focused on what might make them happy *today*; they're focused on their long-term wealth-building plan. I know it sounds like that might be hard to do if you don't naturally think that way, but it's pretty simple: millionaires don't react on impulse, and they don't care about impressing anyone. Instead, they stick to their plans and their principles—and anyone can do that with determination and grit. We found that 97% of millionaires say they almost always achieve the goals they set for themselves. These hardworking people understand the purpose—and the power—of a goal.

92% of millionaires develop a long-term plan for their money, compared to **60%** of the general population.

If they're bold enough to set a goal for themselves, you can bet they're going to take that goal seriously. In fact, 98% of millionaires—practically all of them—say they do not leave things undone and always finish what they start. They may not enter into a commitment lightly, but when they commit, you can count on them to see it through to the end. And that's why they're all millionaires today—they put the goal of financial independence in front of themselves years ago, put a plan in place to reach that goal, and didn't even think of quitting until the job was done.

Guidelines for Goal Setting

There are some incredible books out there that can teach you strategies for goal setting, so I won't go too deep into *how* you set goals. I can, at least, give you a few handy tips to get started.

Mix It Up

First, you need to have a mix of long-term *and* short-term goals. The long-term goals are the ones with huge payoffs, like hitting the $1 million net-worth mark or paying off your house. I love long-term goals, because those are the ones that really move the needle. Changing your life and your family's legacy doesn't happen overnight; that's the result of years and decades of focused intensity. So your biggest goals will be long-term, way off in the distance.

As important as these big goals are, though, you also need to regularly add in short-term goals. You can't expect to stay motivated throughout a twenty-, thirty-, or forty-year journey unless you're seeing wins all along the way. These wins come from short-term goals, such as saving up for a great vacation or buying a car with cash. Knocking out short-term goals gives you a sense of accomplishment and encouragement as you continue to attack your long-term goals. It lets you see that your plan is working, even if you don't have a $1 million net worth yet.

Write Them Down

Second, your goals need to be written down, not just floating around in your head. If they're in your head, they're still hopes and dreams; they don't really become goals until you take the bold step of putting them on paper. That simple act has a huge payoff, too. Dr. Gail Matthews, a psychology professor who conducted a research study on goal setting, found that we are 42% more likely to achieve our goals just by writing them down.[24] There's something about the act of putting goals down on paper that instantly gives a sense of accountability and commitment. It's as though we're taking our dreams out of the clouds and bringing them into the real world. And once they're *real*, it's up to us to go about the hard work of making them happen.

Set SMART Goals

Third, your goals need to be SMART goals. This is an acronym authors and teachers have used for decades to teach people how to set good, well-thought-out goals. For your goals to be SMART, they need to be:

- *Specific*: Leave no room for ambiguity. Write out exactly what you want to accomplish in detail. This is where your high-definition retirement dream comes into play.
- *Measurable*: How will you know if you achieved your goals? Use specific facts, milestones, and metrics so you'll know for sure if you're hitting your goals or not.
- *Achievable*: Be realistic with your goals. Sure, we all want to be billionaires, but that's unlikely for most people. Hitting millionaire status, though, is totally achievable. I want you to dream big, but not so big that you'll never be able to accomplish your goals.
- *Relevant*: Your goals need to be focused. They need to take you closer to where you ultimately want to end up. Having a few

random goals here and there is fine for variety, but your big goals need to work together to bring you into the life you've envisioned for yourself.

* *Time-Sensitive*: Every goal needs a deadline. Challenge yourself to get the job done by a specific date. In retirement planning, for example, this could be the age when you want to retire. And don't be scared to make the timeline ambitious. You'll be amazed how efficiently you can work toward your goals when you know you have a deadline coming up.

Now, let's see what this looks like in practice. Assume you want to pay off your mortgage early. You wouldn't simply write, "I want to pay my house off early" and leave it at that. That goal isn't SMART; it's dumb! It's missing at least two key ingredients: specifics and a deadline. To make your goal SMART, you need to hit all five points by writing something like, "I want to pay off my house in eight years by sending an additional $500 per month toward the principal balance." That goal tells you what you're going to do, when you're going to do it, and how you're going to do it. That's a great goal—and, incidentally, it's one I'm going to challenge you to set for yourself a little later in this chapter.

Setting Goals for Your Money

High-achieving, proactive people set goals in every area of their lives. That includes setting goals for their health, spiritual growth, career, relationships, education, and, of course, finances, just to name a few. While I want you to excel in every part of your life, the focus of this book is to set you on the path to achieving millionaire status. With that in mind, let's focus the rest of this goal-setting discussion on your *financial* goals. Sure, you can apply the following tips to other goals, but I'm going to frame them in terms of your money. If you've never set clear goals for your money before, it's your time to start.

Dave Ramsey's book *The Total Money Makeover* outlines seven crystal-clear financial milestones that should be at the heart of any successful financial plan. If you aren't familiar with Dave's 7 Baby Steps, here's a quick review:

1. Baby Step 1: Save $1,000 for your starter emergency fund.
2. Baby Step 2: Pay off all debt (except the house) using the debt snowball.
3. Baby Step 3: Save 3–6 months of expenses in a fully funded emergency fund.
4. Baby Step 4: Invest 15% of your household income in retirement.
5. Baby Step 5: Save for your children's college fund.
6. Baby Step 6: Pay off your home early.
7. Baby Step 7: Build wealth and give.

I love that Dave's Baby Steps provide several sequential financial goals. When you follow the plan, you know exactly what step you're working on and what comes next.

You'll see that several of these steps involve saving money. That's crucial. This may sound like an obvious point by now, but I need to say it anyway: *millionaires save money.* They don't spend everything they make, and they have a plan for what they want their money to do. In fact, we found that 70% of millionaires saved more than 10% of their income throughout their working years. Thirty percent of them saved more than 20% of their income. When we asked what factors contributed to their net worth, 83%

> **70%** of millionaires saved more than **10%** of their income throughout their working years.

said saving money. If you want to be a millionaire, you've *got to* save money. You may be thinking, *Chris, how in the world can I do that? I make a modest salary and big unexpected expenses always seem to come up!* You need an emergency fund to cover those; get that in place first. That way, you're in control when life throws something at you. Once your debt is all paid off and you have a full emergency fund with three to six months of expenses, you need to invest at least 15% of your income toward retirement while you work to pay off your house. Remember, millionaires don't sit around and wait for one giant payday that's going to solve all their problems. They save money every payday, and they put that money to work for them. It takes hard work, but you can do it. Remember, setting the goal and sticking to it are half the battle!

As you work through the Baby Steps, you'll find that the first three steps can happen a lot faster than the last four. Baby Steps 1, 2, and 3 are short-term goals; many people can go from neck-deep in debt to debt-free with an emergency fund in two or three years on average. From there, they hit the often-frustrating stretch of long-term goals. These are the things most people spend ten or more years working toward, and that kind of far-off vision takes a lot of commitment, not to mention patience. To make the road a little smoother, here are some strategies for finishing your financial marathon with gusto.

Visualize Results

Get a clear picture of where you want to go. This goes back to the dream meeting I talked about. You (and your spouse if you're married) need to know exactly what you're working toward. And, like your goals, you need to write this vision down. It may be the only thing that keeps you going on days when your energy is down, the road seems long, and the effort doesn't seem worth it. In those times, you'll need to remind yourself why you're working so hard to begin with.

Break Down Your Goals

Breaking through the $1 million net-worth barrier is an enormous goal that can seem insurmountable at times. That's why I recommend breaking your big goals down into smaller, more manageable short-term goals. These are the milestones, the mini-victories that will ultimately deliver you to the big win you're chasing. If you want $2 million in your retirement accounts by age sixty, for example, you can use the R:IQ tool I mentioned earlier to figure out exactly how much you need to save every month. With that one action, you'll break a huge $2 million goal into smaller, less-intimidating monthly goals.

Track Your Progress

Once you've got a plan in place and settle into the long haul of working toward it, it can be easy to lose track of where you are on the journey. Instead, stay focused. The best way to do this is to recalculate your net worth every month or two. You could even create a visual chart to track your progress on your way to the big goal. Whether it's a boring spreadsheet or a giant poster hanging in your house, figure out some way to track your progress and look at it regularly for motivation. Having a tracking system enables you to quickly see how far you've come and motivates you to find new ways to move further faster.

Reward Yourself

Celebrating your accomplishments should not be a once-and-for-all event when you finally hit financial independence. Instead, you need to build in incremental milestones and reward yourself for reaching them. No, I'm not saying you should spend $100 for every $200 you save. However, there's nothing wrong with saying, "When my net worth hits $250,000, I'm taking my family to Disney World to celebrate!" Stopping to celebrate the small wins will keep you excited about pushing through to the next milestone, and all those little victories add up over time!

Get Encouragement

Sometimes even the most motivated person starts to lose faith that the sacrifices are worth the effort. That's when we need some encouragement from people who have met and conquered the obstacles we're still up against. This is where the mentor and cheerleader we discussed in chapter 6 come into play. Or you could use millionaire success stories, such as the ones in this book and the ones on the Millionaire Theme Hour of *The Dave Ramsey Show*, to keep your motivation up. Whatever the source, find something or someone who will keep your spirits high and your eyes fixed on the goal.

Learn from Winners

We've seen that building wealth isn't *easy* per se, but it's also not that complicated. Most of the millionaires we studied built their wealth by doing the same simple things—such as investing in their company retirement plan—over and over again for an extended period of time. That simplicity, however, doesn't mean there aren't more things to learn. You can stay motivated and make even stronger strides toward your millionaire goal by learning tips and tools to take your wealth building to the next level. Books, mastermind groups, and investing classes are fantastic resources to keep your tools sharp. Just be careful not to be pulled off course by a risky "opportunity" that could endanger your millionaire goals.

LONG-TERM WEALTH GOALS

As you begin to set goals for your financial future, there are a few key areas you should focus on right off the bat. Again, these are long-term goals, but you can't put them off. Building wealth is a long-term *play*, but it can't be a long-term *delay*. The actions and steps you take today will shape what kind of life you'll have twenty or thirty years from now. So let's make sure you're doing everything you can to get your future financial house in order.

But First . . .

One quick word before we dive into these long-term goals. I want you to start working on these things as soon as possible, but not before you're ready. That means you need to be out of debt (except for the house) and have a fully funded emergency fund of three to six months' worth of expenses in the bank. If you haven't hit those two goals yet, that should be your focus right now. Trying to build wealth while dragging around a car note and student loan payments is like trying to run a marathon with an anchor tied around your ankle. All that debt will do is slow you down and split your efforts. Get your immediate financial situation in good shape first, and then move on to the long-term goals we're about to discuss. Got it?

Invest for Long-Term Wealth Building

The main long-term goal as you work toward financial independence is to invest wisely. Remember, the millionaires we studied didn't build their wealth in risky investments, sophisticated market strategies, or crazy real estate schemes. More millionaires say the 401(k) has played the largest role in building their net worth compared to other investing products. In fact, the 401(k) has made more of a difference than basic saving, real estate, inheritance, and selling a business *combined*. Focusing on that slow-and-steady, long-term goal isn't always easy, though. Building wealth requires personal responsibility, intentionality, and goals—not to mention sacrifice. But you—yes, *you*—have what it takes. In order to invest, you must make daily decisions to not spend your money on something fun or flashy, something that would make your life more enjoyable *today*. Although it can be difficult in the moment, it's really that simple. And when you invest, you're choosing an unbelievably awesome future over a marginally improved present.

Millionaires work hard for their money, but they also know how to let their money work hard for them. That only happens when you inject some discipline into your budget and make whatever sacrifices you need to make in the short term to free up money to invest for the long term. That echoes the advice that Will, one of the millionaires we interviewed in our study, gave to us. "Not having a plan to become a millionaire will keep people from ever becoming one," he warns. Becoming a millionaire is a goal, and it's a goal Will worked toward for most of his life.

EVERYDAY MILLIONAIRE

Will—a millionaire from Chicago—grew up in a blue-collar family and always watched his parents struggle with money. Seeing their constant money stress pushed Will to pursue financial independence for himself when he graduated college. He started out as a history teacher, but when he saw that accounting offered a more likely path to his financial goals, he went back to school to earn an accounting degree. He took an accounting job when he graduated, and he stayed with that same company for thirty-one years, eventually working his way up to the chief financial officer position. He married early in his career, and he and his wife, Holly, shared the goal of complete financial independence. Throughout their marriage, they lived frugally and drove older cars despite good incomes. They also prioritized saving and investing in their 401(k)s and other investments.

As the 401(k) plan administrator for his company, Will saw how other employees failed to take advantage of the simple wealth-building tools at their disposal. He knew everyone's salary, and he was shocked and saddened to see that they weren't investing much, if anything, into the company 401(k)—despite the generous company match. "People would rather spend money than save money," he says. That, plus the instant-gratification mentality he sees all around him, is why he thinks most people don't hit the millionaire mark. By avoiding these traps and keeping their long-term goals in mind, Will and Holly are now enjoying their dream retirement with a net worth of nearly $4.5 million—something his parents couldn't have imagined.

Build a Bridge

One thing that often gets overlooked by a lot of future millionaires is the *bridge period*. That's what I call the period between the time you stop working and the time you're able to start withdrawing funds from your retirement accounts. If you plan to retire early, this warning is for you. Let's say you want to retire at age fifty-five. That's great—but only if you've planned for it. You can't withdraw funds from your retirement accounts without incurring a penalty until you're age fifty-nine and a half, so in this example, you'll need about four and a half years of investment savings outside of your retirement accounts to live on.

While I and almost all the millionaires we talked to love the 401(k) and similar retirement accounts, you need to plan for a little extra to cover your bridge years. For this, I recommend setting some money aside in a good growth-stock mutual fund outside of your retirement accounts. As you plan your retirement dream, simply set a retirement age target, figure out how much money you'll need to live on, and make sure you're on track to have that much set aside for each year of your early retirement until you can access your retirement accounts without penalty. This shouldn't be intimidating, but it can be a little tricky. I suggest working with both an investment and a tax professional to make sure this part of your plan is locked in tight.

THE BIG GOAL: PAY OFF YOUR HOUSE

For most people, paying off their home mortgage is the last massive hurdle in reaching financial independence. However, millionaires think differently because they know that "normal" too often means "broke." They know that thinking differently and actually doing the math cause money to stay with them and grow instead of leaving them to go to others. Think about it: How would it feel to not have a house payment for the first time in your life? Most people sign up for thirty-year mortgages in their twenties or thirties and never stop to imagine what it would be like if they didn't have that huge monthly payment hanging over their heads every month. They think it's simply part of life. That's a straight-up lie. Throughout the rest of this chapter on goal-setting, I want to challenge you to set one of the most significant, gratifying, and wealth-building goals you can imagine: paying off your house for good. I want to challenge you to think differently—radically—and begin to see how paying off your home can actually help you achieve millionaire status!

It took the average millionaire 10.2 years to pay off their homes, and **67%** of them live in homes with paid-off mortgages.

The Typical Millionaire Home

Earlier in this book, I asked you to imagine what a "millionaire" looks like, including how they act, what they drive, how they dress, and where they live. If you started with images of Richie Rich and Scrooge McDuck in your head, it's time to wake up. We've seen over and over that millionaires are regular people—and now I want you to know that these successful men and women live in *regular* homes.

According to our research, the average millionaire lives in a 2,600-square-foot house that they've lived in for seventeen years. Depending on what part of the country you live in, that could sound gigantic. However, the average square footage of all homes built in 2015 is 2,687.[25] That means, despite their wealth, millionaires live in average-sized homes that they've lived in for a long time. These aren't super-fancy neighborhoods, either. Nearly one-third of millionaires live in a ZIP code where home values are below the national average ($205,000 or less), and 51% live in neighborhoods where the average household income is $75,000 or less. Like I've been saying, these are regular people who live in predominately average houses. Millionaires don't feel the need to upgrade, and they aren't looking for bigger and better simply because they can afford it. Instead, they stay put and actually pay the darn things off.

We found that it took millionaires an average of 10.2 years to pay off their homes, and 67% of them live in homes with paid off mortgages. This is important, because it puts their home entirely in the asset column of their net worth *and* it wipes their biggest debt off the liability column. On average, one-third of a millionaire's net worth comes from their primary residence. So, if you're sitting in a paid-for $350,000 home, that entire $350,000 counts toward your net worth. If you've got that plus $650,000 in retirement accounts, you're a millionaire!

Mortgage Games

Thirty-year mortgages dominate the home loan industry. And I mean *dominate*. Why is this? Well, it's pretty simple. The thirty-year mortgage is what makes banks and mortgage companies the most money! So, of course, that's the term of mortgage they are going to promote, market, and offer to consumers. Freddie Mac reports that

90% of all homebuyers choose a thirty-year mortgage when buying a house.[26] Only 6% of buyers select a fifteen-year loan.[27] This absolutely blows my mind. If you want to know why most people don't become millionaires, look no further than the thirty-year mortgage. People throw away tens—even hundreds—of thousands of dollars on these loans without ever stopping to do the math. If you've never faced the numbers, buckle up. It's time for me to make you hate your mortgage.

Let's look at a $225,000 mortgage at 4% interest, for example. If you, like nine out of ten buyers, went with the thirty-year mortgage, your payment (principal and interest) would be $1,074. If you went with a fifteen-year mortgage, your payment would be $1,664—$590 more per month. Look, I get it. Saving $590 every month sounds great, but that's a short-term view. We're looking out in the distance and setting long-term goals now, remember? So, let's see what that $590 a month savings actually *costs* you. After ten years, the balance on the thirty-year loan would be $177,264. You would have paid a total of $128,880 on the thirty-year mortgage, but you only would have knocked $47,736 off the principal balance. That means you would have thrown away more than $81,000 in interest payments just in the first ten years—and you'd still have twenty years to go!

Compare that to the fifteen-year loan at the ten-year mark. Your balance would be $90,369, and you would have paid $65,049 in interest. Sure, that's still a lot of interest, but don't miss a few things:

- You *still* would have paid less in interest.
- You would have paid off almost twice as much of the principal balance.
- You'd only have five years left to go!

And these numbers only represent what's going on at the ten-year mark of these loans. If you really need more convincing that the fifteen-year mortgage is the way to go, then let's see how much money would have gone to interest over the entire course of the loans. The thirty-year mortgage would have cost you a grand total of $161,640 in interest. That's money you basically would have given away to the bank for the pleasure of doing business with them. That's $161,640 that you wouldn't have had going toward your net worth or into your investments. Compare that to the fifteen-year loan. With that option, you would have had to come up with $590 more per month, but you'd be finished with the payments fifteen years sooner *and* you only would have paid $74,520 in interest—more than $87,000 less than the thirty-year loan would have cost you! So, just in this example, going against the flow and choosing a fifteen-year loan would have saved you more than $87,000 and would have put you in a paid-for home in half the time. How on earth can anyone look at this and *still* choose a thirty-year mortgage? I may have answered my own question: *no one* ever looks at this. Well, no one except your average millionaire, that is.

So, if you really want to become a millionaire, then you need to start acting like one. We told you earlier that it took millionaires an average of 10.2 years to pay off their homes. How quickly could you pay off yours if you got super serious about it? What would it take? Well, I'll tell you. It would take a little planning, a big goal, and a lot of commitment over an extended period of time. So remember, at this point you're investing 15% of your income in tax-favored retirement plans and you're saving for college (if you have kids). Once you have those two things in motion, you need to look at your budget and figure out what you have left over. Any extra money you can squeeze out of your budget—and I mean everything but the kitchen sink—should go straight toward paying off your mortgage. This is not the time to take your foot off the gas. This is the very last debt standing in your way of being completely debt-free! Don't stop now. Make every penny count. Now *that's* acting like a millionaire!

Avoid Mortgage Traps

Besides dragging out a mortgage longer than necessary, there are two other huge mortgage-related mistakes that can drive your millionaire aspirations off a cliff. First is the belief that you should keep your mortgage because of the tax advantages. People ask, "Why would I want to pay off my mortgage? I get a great tax break by writing off the mortgage interest." I can't believe how many people think this is a good idea. Can these people not do basic math? Here's the deal: yes, you get to write off your mortgage interest on your tax return, but that write-off will never save you more than it *costs* you. Here's a quick example: if you have a $200,000 loan at a 5% interest rate, you'll pay $10,000 a year in interest. Because mortgage interest is tax-deductible, you get to write off that amount, meaning you won't pay income tax on that $10,000. If you're in a 25% tax bracket, that deduction will save you $2,500 a year in taxes. Well, all right. Who doesn't want to save $2,500 in taxes? Case closed, right? Wrong.

If that's as far as you take it, you can fool yourself into thinking it's a smart thing to keep the mortgage just for the tax deduction. You need to open your eyes, though, and see the bigger picture. In that example, you sent the bank $10,000, and that enabled you to save $2,500 off your tax bill. Don't miss that: you *traded* $10,000 for $2,500. That's like asking a cashier to break a $10 bill for you, but he only gives back $2.50—and you *thank him for it.* If you want to build wealth, you have to be smarter than that. Wealthy people know that it's better to save the whole $10,000! Of course, you absolutely should take advantage of the tax deduction as long as you have a mortgage—that's smart! But don't use that deduction as an excuse to keep the mortgage any longer than necessary.

The second mortgage-related mistake that can completely derail your millionaire goals is the home equity line of credit. Oh, the HELOC! This little gem has gotten a lot of attention over the past twenty years or so. But as I said in chapter 3, the HELOC is nothing more than a second mortgage. Worse, it's a second mortgage tied to an easy-access debit card that enables you to chip away at your home's equity one vacation or kitchen upgrade at a time. A HELOC basically takes two incredibly stupid ideas—a second mortgage and a credit card—and jams them together into one destructive opportunity to sabotage your financial independence. Don't fall for the sales pitch. This isn't a tool of the wealthy; it's a crutch for the broke and ignorant. Remember, 63% of millionaires have *never* taken out a home equity loan or line of credit, and only 9% of millionaires currently have a home equity loan. The majority of millionaires don't fall for this garbage, and neither should you.

Make Yourself Rich—Not the Bank or Mortgage Company

Stop and dream for a minute. What would life be like if you didn't have to send $1,500 or $2,000 to the bank every month for the next twenty years? What could you do? What difference would that extra income make for you, your family, and your community? What impact would it have on the legacy you're building, on the financial dream you're imagining? If you planned, worked, and sacrificed to pay your thirty-year mortgage off in only ten years, you would give yourself twenty extra years of wealth-building power. Let's say your mortgage payment was $1,500 a month. If you paid the house off in ten years and invested that $1,500 a month for the next twenty years, that investment alone would make you a millionaire with $1,134,000. And, going back to what we learned about compound interest, 68% of that $1.1 million would be growth—that is, interest that you earned over and above the money you actually put in. Even better, at that point you would also have a paid-for home with thirty years of appreciation on top of that $1.1 million. You'd be a net-worth millionaire, and that doesn't even count what you'd have in your retirement accounts by then. At that point you'd be like David, a retired college professor and millionaire our team interviewed.

EVERYDAY MILLIONAIRE ———————————————————————

David, a millionaire from Oklahoma, was born to parents who taught him the basics of money management from an early age. His father was an engineer, and his mother was a schoolteacher. Together, his parents made enough to meet the needs of the family, but David remembers them as frugal. They taught him how to save money and the importance of staying away from debt—two lessons that shaped his financial future. After high school, David went on to pursue a bachelor's degree in civil engineering and a PhD in aerospace engineering. He settled into a long, thirty-five-year career as a college professor and, in his spare time, started two different software companies. All these things were in pursuit of a goal he'd had most of his life: to become financially independent.

David learned early in his working life that there is a big difference between wealth and income. He figured out that his income could either come from a *job* or from his *wealth*, and he set his sights on a wealth-based income stream, picturing a day when his investments would support the life he and his wife dreamed of. To make that dream a reality, they maximized their 401(k), 403(b), and IRAs. They carefully considered other opportunities as they came along, always weighing the risk against the long-term goal they were chasing. They also used an investment professional to help make the best investing decisions throughout their working lifetime.

Today, David has crushed his goal of financial independence. With a net worth of $2.2 million, he and his wife have not one but *two* paid-for houses, spending part of the year in their Colorado vacation home. David still works, but he does it for fun and only part time. When we asked him what he tells his students about building wealth, he said he always points back to the goals he had early on. He explained that most people have unrealistic expectations of retirement and eventually find themselves unprepared. You can't enjoy retirement or reach financial independence, he warns, if you don't plan ahead. "You need to know how much you want to spend—and then you need to make sure you have more saved than you plan to spend when you get there." Simple advice that, I hate to say, too many people just don't—or won't—follow.

WORKING TOWARD MILLIONAIRE GOALS

Again, *anyone* can become a millionaire in this country, but it won't happen by accident. It takes time, intentionality, a little financial intelligence, and goals. If you have those things, anything's possible. Understand that a goal is simply a promise you make to yourself. I hope by now that you've made that promise, that you have accepted the call to join the ranks of America's millionaires. It may seem like a lofty goal to set, but trust me, it's possible. My purpose in this chapter has been to get you to start picturing that millionaire life for yourself and to help you set some long-term goals to get there. If you take these things to heart, I know you can cross that millionaire finish line. Too many people look at the challenges and distractions all around us and ask, "How can I ever become a millionaire?" That's not your question, though. From now on, I want you to start asking yourself, "*How soon* can I become a millionaire?" Equipped with your new mind-set, you can start setting those short- and long-term goals that will get you there.

Millionaires Do

- **Set goals.** 92% of millionaires develop a long-term plan for their money, compared to 60% of the general population.

- **Accomplish their goals.** 97% of millionaires say they almost always achieve the goals they set for themselves.

- **Save consistently.** 70% of millionaires save more than 10% of their income throughout their working years.

Millionaires Don't

- **Live in mansions.** *The average millionaire has lived in the same 2,600-square-foot house for the past seventeen years.*

- **Keep their home mortgages for the tax advantage.** *It took the millionaires an average of 10.2 years to pay off their homes, and 67% of them live in homes with paid-off mortgages.*

I grew up on welfare. My siblings never finished school. I was on my own at age fourteen and self-supporting. Hard work, saving, education, and a positive attitude always landed me in very good jobs where I continued to save. I had a mind-set that I couldn't count on family, so I had better take care of myself. I was blessed to be able to financially care for my mother (now deceased) who had nothing at retirement. If a poor kid who came from welfare can become a millionaire, anyone can do it.

—JIM, $2.8 MILLION NET WORTH

Chapter 9

Do What It Takes

Millionaires Are Hard Workers

As we've poured through our research on America's millionaires, we haven't seen any big educational or intellectual advantages. We have not seen huge inheritances or lottery payouts. We haven't seen crazy, strike-it-rich, once-in-a-lifetime, risky investments. You know what we have seen? Work. Lots and lots of meticulous, often grueling and gritty, dirt-under-the-fingernails, nose-to-the-grindstone, hard work. Wherever they are and whatever they're doing, these men and women work with intensity—and all that hard work has paid off.

Have you noticed how many of the millionaire stories we've seen in this book contain the word *farm*? I have. I swear, it seems like every other millionaire we've featured grew up on a farm. I don't think that's an accident. There's no such thing as a lazy farmer. Farms require you to put in the work day in and day out. If you stop or even slow down, you could ruin whole crops. You could end up with nothing to sell—or eat. A farm background develops the solid, life-long work ethic that's required to build wealth. I understand that; I actually worked on a farm myself when I was a teenager. I bailed and loaded hay, worked in the barn, and kept up the property for a huge farm back in Kentucky. I remember taking the weed trimmer to a mile-long stretch of fence in one pasture, knowing I'd have another, bigger pasture to deal with the next day. The work never stopped, and if I slowed down, I knew all that work would overtake me. But at the end of a long day, I used to love sitting back and just looking at the fields I had worked. I could see the progress and the payoff. I could tell exactly how my work made a difference that day. My fingerprints were all over that farm, and I was proud to contribute to its success.

My farming experience as a teenager made such an impact on me that I'm looking for farm jobs for my three sons this summer. They may not enjoy every aspect of all the hard work, but they're going to learn the value of a good day's work under the sun. They're going to learn what I—and the millionaires in our study—have learned: your commitment to hard work will shape the course of your life forever.

MILLIONAIRES WORK HARD

I've heard excuses from so many people about why they *can't* get ahead financially. They whine, "I don't have enough time" or "I'm not smart enough" or "My job doesn't pay enough." Whenever I hear this garbage, I always tell people it's not about how much time you have, how smart you are, or how much you make; it's about what you do with what you have and how hard you're willing to work. That's usually when someone will come back with the excuse that *really* burns me up: "But, Chris, you don't want me to become a workaholic, do you?" Oh, please.

I've said over and over in this book that *anyone* can become a millionaire in America today, but I may need to clarify that a bit.

I believe *anyone who's willing to work hard* can become a millionaire in America today. The average millionaire agrees with me, as 76% say that, with hard work and discipline, anyone can become a millionaire. Does that mean you need to work eighty hours a week, forsake your family, and destroy your health chasing wealth? No way. But do I think you can work better, smarter, and more efficiently in the forty hours you're already working? Absolutely. Remember, only 7% of the millionaires we studied are C-suite executives, meaning they have a high-paying Chief *Something* Officer title. And 93% of millionaires said they built wealth by hard work rather than big salaries. These people aren't looking for the government or anyone else to take care of them, and they certainly aren't sitting around griping about why "the little man can't get ahead." Millionaire-minded people don't have time for that kind of self-pity; they're too busy working!

76% of millionaires say that anyone can become a millionaire with hard work and discipline.

Hard Work Disguised as Luck

Ninety-nine percent of millionaires said their friends and family members would describe them as hard workers. This is the behind-the-scenes reality that most people never consider when they think about how a typical millionaire built their wealth. The truth is, hard work looks like luck to the outside world. In fact, I'd say that hard work is practically *invisible* to those who don't work hard themselves. They can't picture themselves sacrificing and saving for twenty or thirty years straight, so they think no one else can either. What some people see as luck is just a matter of discipline, sacrifice, persistence, and good old-fashioned hard work—which sounds a lot like Pam, one of the hardworking millionaires we interviewed.

EVERYDAY MILLIONAIRE

Pam's parents struggled financially for most of her childhood, but throughout that time, she was blessed with a hardworking father who worked his way up from the mail room to a factory manager position for a phone company. While he always made a lower-middle-class income with just enough for their basic needs, Pam's father consistently taught her the value of hard work and self-sufficiency. Now retired and with a net worth of nearly $2 million, Pam can still hear his voice echoing in her head, "Don't look to someone else to get something you can get for yourself . . . [and] don't work harder at getting *out* of work than actually working."

Those are lessons she learned and applied from a young age. With no money for college after high school, Pam went to work and saved for her own tuition. She started college at age twenty and worked on her degree steadily, as her income allowed, for eleven years before graduating at age thirty-one. During that time, she purchased a home, saved for retirement, got married, had three kids, and even paid for her husband's college degree. From age nineteen, Pam saved 10% of every dollar she earned, putting the power of compound interest—what she calls the "Eighth Wonder of the World"—to work for her. She lived below her means, never drove a new car, and stayed away from debt. When she lost a good bit of money in an unfortunate divorce from her first husband in her mid-forties, Pam picked herself back up and kept herself and her goals on track. Even though she was starting again from zero, she never gave up, never slowed down, and never stopped working for what she wanted to accomplish. Now remarried, Pam recently sold a company she built from the ground up and is enjoying a wonderful retirement filled with traveling, visiting art exhibitions, writing poetry, and going scuba diving whenever she wants. But don't think this retired millionaire has gotten lazy. She's still working to improve herself by taking college classes in her retirement. That's the thing about people who aren't scared to work hard. Even when they retire, they're still looking for ways to learn, work, and grow.

Learning How to Work

Pam's story resonates with me. I think her father and my grandfather would have gotten along. I spent a lot of time with my grandparents as a kid, and my grandfather taught me the value and dignity in a good day's work. This guy was tireless. He was up at 3:00 a.m. every day to go work in a factory. He'd get home late in the afternoon, eat some dinner, change his clothes, and then move on to some project around the house. I'd find him under a car, up on the roof, painting a bedroom—wherever there was work to be done, my grandfather was there doing it. He never seemed to get tired, and he never sat still for too long. He was a man of few words, but no one ever taught me more about the value of work than he did. I can't quote any catchy one-liner or specific piece of advice he gave me about work, though. He *taught* me by *showing* me. It's a lesson that's shaped my life.

Maybe you had a parent or grandparent like that. You know, someone who was always shuffling around from one task to another, teaching you by their words and actions what it meant to work hard. I've heard things like, "If a job's worth doing, it's worth doing right." Or maybe, "It's always easier to do a job right the first time than to redo it a second time." Or, one of my favorites, "Don't do anything halfway. Either do the whole job or don't bother." These little bits of wisdom aren't simply "dad speak." They actually go back hundreds and thousands of years. Ben Franklin was thought to have said, "Motivation is when your dreams put on work clothes," and Thomas Edison is known for the adage, "Opportunity is missed by most people because it's dressed in overalls and looks like work." The Bible even has plenty to say about work, such as, "All hard work brings a profit, but mere talk leads only to poverty" (Proverbs 14:23). These timeless pieces of wisdom point to the inescapable fact that work—and our attitude about work—matters more than we might think.

BUILDING A STRONG WORK ETHIC

Too many people view their jobs as a weight around their necks. They think their lives happen on the weekends and that their Monday through Friday work is the necessary evil required for a paycheck. That's a terrible way to go through life, and it's something that's completely foreign to most millionaires. An unbelievable 96% of net-worth millionaires enjoyed what they did for a career. Sixty-four percent took it a step further and said they loved their jobs. They must love them, because 56% are still working in some capacity *even though* they've achieved financial independence. In fact, more than one-third (37%) are still working full time. Why? Because they enjoy their work and they find fulfillment in it. Of all the millionaires we talked to, only 38% were fully retired.

96% of millionaires enjoyed what they did for a career, and **64%** say they "loved" their jobs.

Why do millionaires like to work so much? I think it's because a strong work ethic has been grafted into their DNA. They work because they *like* to work; it's who they are. They've learned to see the moral good in a day's work, and they don't want to lose that sense of accomplishment just so they can sit on a beach sipping fruity drinks every day until they die of boredom. That's not who they were while they were building wealth, and it's not who they are now that they've become financially independent.

Hard Work in Action

When I think about the key characteristics of a strong work ethic—things like dedication, grit, discipline, self-control, dependability, and character—I think of Mitch, a millionaire we talked to from Ohio.

EVERYDAY MILLIONAIRE

Mitch learned his incredible work ethic from his dad while working the two-hundred-acre family farm. That's right—*another* farm-bred millionaire. They'd work side by side all day, and Mitch was amazed at how his dad managed to outwork everyone else. "It was hard work," Mitch said, "but it taught us a lot of good values, such as how to run a business, how to make money, and how to get ahead."

Mitch put those lessons to use early in life. He excelled at academics and sports in high school, and he learned that he could do anything that he set his mind to and was willing to work for. After graduating at the top of his class, he started college and developed a passion for flying. He earned his pilot's license with the intention of flying commercially, but he had a hard time finding a pilot position out of school. He took a job as an air traffic controller instead, staying there for eleven years—until a massive industry strike cost him his job and forced him to find a new line of work. After weighing his options, Mitch decided to return to the family farm, which has since grown to eight hundred acres. He also began investing in real estate, building up a portfolio of thirty-five properties. Never wanting to worry about losing his job again, Mitch focused on building multiple income streams. He told us one of the keys to his long-term success has been working in two or three different businesses over many years.

Mitch taught himself the basics of investing in his late thirties to make the best use of his income. He invested in a 401(k) and an IRA in addition to his real estate investments. His wife, Leah, has also worked throughout their entire marriage. She started investing into her company's retirement plan at age twenty-five—jumping into the 401(k) when that rolled out—and worked there for forty years. She made the 401(k) a priority that entire time, and she and Mitch never even considered borrowing against it or withdrawing it early—even during Mitch's career change. Today, Leah has $1 million in her 401(k). The couple would be millionaires on her 401(k) alone, but that's just one piece of this incredible couple's wealth. When you add that to Mitch's accounts, the eight-hundred-acre farm, and thirty-five properties, they have a total net worth of $9 million. These two have absolutely killed it through their intense focus and hard work.

Mitch's dad always told him, "Isn't it funny how the people who work the hardest are the 'luckiest' people?" That incredible work ethic has fueled Mitch and Leah's success for decades, and now they are living the "luckiest" life of their dreams. The couple still works hard, but they do it on their terms and only as much (or little) as they want to. They play hard, too, taking at least five separate two-week vacations a year, and often moving into their Florida vacation home for weeks at a time. That's the kind of life you can live if you're not scared to work hard to reach your goals.

Benefits of a Strong Work Ethic

A nice, paid-for Florida vacation home is awesome, but it's not the biggest benefit you can gain from a strong work ethic. There are many more important advantages that will make you a better, more stable, more profitable person no matter what business you're in. First, a commitment to hard work builds patience. Reaching financial independence takes a long time. As we saw in chapter 3, the average millionaire hit the $1 million mark at 49 years old. That means it took *decades* of slugging it out day after day for most of these families to hit their goal! The ability to work hard over a long period of time builds patience like nothing else will. It keeps you focused so you never lose sight of what you're striving toward.

Second, a good work ethic enables you to experience progress. Your work should take you a little closer to your ultimate goal every single day. Every paycheck, every 401(k) or other retirement account contribution, every promotion—they're all individual steps on your journey to financial independence. And little by little, as you check your progress and factor in your net worth, you're able to see that you are moving the needle.

Third, work gives you a sense of accomplishment. The old expression, "An honest day's work for an honest day's pay" means something. It feels good to get a paycheck for a job well done, doesn't it? Just imagine how you'll feel when your income comes solely from your investments that you've worked, saved, and sacrificed for. Although it seems far off now, those incremental investments from your paychecks add up over time. Never forget that you are building a perpetual stream of income in your investing accounts; every dollar you save and invest today will become part of your income later. Saving enough money to live on for the rest of your life is a huge deal, so be proud of every step you take toward that goal.

Fourth, good work continually builds your self-confidence. It shows us what we're capable of and reminds us what we've accomplished so far. Consider that for a minute. Think back to a job you had to perform or a big task you had to accomplish—something that scared the crap out of you and that you thought was impossible. Do you remember how intimidating that task was on day one? For me, it was writing my first book. I had never done it before, and the thought of writing one hundred thousand words (that actually made sense) stressed me out. But I got to work. I knocked out the first chapter, then the second. I kept plodding through it, working with the team that had come around me. Within a few months, I had a finished manuscript. The "impossible" task was done. I had tamed the monster. From that point on and for the rest of my life, I know that I'm capable of writing a book—because I've done it. That sense of self-confidence is one of my favorite benefits of hard work.

Fifth, hard work makes an impact on your career. This fifth benefit seems like a no-brainer, but don't overlook it. Working hard isn't just about doing your job. It's more than your paycheck; it's also about where you are, the work you're doing, what you're contributing, who you're doing it with, and the greater mission you're helping your company accomplish. You're showing who you are, what you have to offer, and whether or not the people around you can trust you to do what you say you're going to do. Remember, 96% of millionaires said they enjoyed what they did for a career, and 99% said the people around them would describe them as a hard worker. When you work hard at a job you enjoy, you unlock all kinds of potential in yourself. That makes you better not just at work, but in every other part of your life, too.

When it comes to your career, you want to strive to become the type of person Patrick Lencioni describes in his book *The Ideal Team Player*: someone who is hungry (a motivated go-getter), humble (knows who they are and what they bring to the table), and smart (expertly manages relationships). Isn't that the kind of person you want to work with? Isn't that who you'd want to hire onto your team? These are the kind of men and women who make a huge impact in the workplace. They get their own work done with excellence, and more impressively, they bring up the game of everyone around them. That's the power of a strong work ethic.

Sixth, as Lencioni noted, hard work builds humility. When you spend years working toward a goal, you understand at a deep level how hard it is and what it takes to achieve something big. You probably also experience enough failure along the way that you lose any arrogance you may have had about the accomplishment. That's something I've noted in most of the millionaires I've known: hard workers usually won't brag about themselves. It's like watching a sportscaster interview an Olympic gold medalist. You can hear the interviewer try to get the athlete to talk a big game, but the best ones won't go there. They'll thank their team members, their coaches, their families, and even God, but I've never heard a star Olympian say, "You know, I always knew I was the best at this sport—and now the world knows it, too. It's about time I got this gold medal." Their years of training and countless hours of practice have knocked those rough edges off. Their hard work doesn't just make them champions, it makes them humble. They know they didn't achieve the victory alone, and they are grateful for the people who supported them, trained them, encouraged them, and sacrificed for them. I don't know about you, but I love being around humble people who just so happen to be the best in the world at what they do. There's nothing like it.

All these benefits work together to completely revolutionize your character. In total, the ability to work hard gives you an advantage, builds your confidence, allows you to experience gratitude, leads to self-improvement, and makes you intentional in all other areas. What I'm saying, then, is that hard work simply makes you better. If you aren't happy with who you are and what you've accomplished so far, I've got good news: better is available. But you'll have to work for it.

HOW TO BETTER YOURSELF
THROUGH HARD WORK

Becoming a well-rounded, financially independent powerhouse takes effort, and that effort may be new to you. Sure, some people may naturally have more energy and grit than others, but that's no excuse for you to sit on your hands and only wish for what other people have. If you have a desire to win, you've got to put that desire to work. Let's look at some practical ways the millionaires we talked to amped up their efforts to achieve the maximum results.

Better Your Mind

I don't care what you do for a living, how many degrees you have, or how smart you think you are, education will make you better at your job. There is *always* more to learn, and millionaire-minded people never stop learning. If you never went to college, you might want to consider it. We found that 88% of millionaires have a college degree. Like we saw in chapter 4, though, the prestige of the school doesn't really matter. The important thing is the education itself, not the name of the school. In fact, you could pick up a few classes at a local community college in your spare time. That would give you access to professional instructors and an accredited curriculum without costing you an arm and a leg.

If you choose to head back to school, remember to stay far, far away from student loans. That's a trap. If you rack up thousands of dollars in debt in an effort to increase your earning potential, you'll just be shooting yourself in the foot. Millionaires (and future millionaires) don't play around with student loans. As we saw in chapter 4, nearly seven out of ten millionaires with a degree graduated without ever taking a penny in student loans. Like I've said before, the cost of higher education has increased in recent years, but remember, you need to avoid student loans like the plague. Paying for your education with student loans will limit your options—both immediately after college and for the long term. Millionaires don't take on debt—and neither should you.

If you don't want to go back to school or can't for whatever reason, you still have plenty of options. Here's an idea: read a book.

You can fit a thousand degrees' worth of reading onto your iPad or Kindle, so get started. The answer to pretty much any question you can imagine is already written in a book somewhere; all you have to do is go find it. You can also dive into trade journals, conferences, classes, online training, mentoring programs, mastermind groups, or a million other educational options. *Education* doesn't necessarily mean a formal degree program or a diploma. You don't need another slip of paper or credential; you need to *learn*. And you can learn anytime, anywhere, anyplace, no matter how much time or money you have today.

Better Your Skill Set

We have a saying around our office: "Your raise is effective when you are." So, if you want to increase your income, you need to invest some time and energy into increasing your skill set. Millionaires aren't content with how well they do their jobs. Rather, we found that 96% are always trying to learn new things. They want to find new ways to do their jobs better. And, of course, as you get better at your job, you produce greater results. This makes you more valuable to your employer and often leads to higher earning potential. You bring a unique set of skills to your work, and anything you can do to make those skills more valuable makes you more valuable to your employer.

96% of millionaires are always trying to learn new things.

Picture your professional skills as a set of tools. They're bright and shiny when you first get them, but over time, they start to wear out. They get rusty. The blades get dull. They aren't as effective as they were when you first started out, and every year new people with brand-new tools start competing for your opportunities. If you want to stay competitive, you have to keep your tools sharp, good as new, and ready to use at a moment's notice.

86% of millionaires believe challenging themselves will make them smarter.

You can sharpen your skill set in a lot of ways. Education, of course, is a no-brainer—but don't just think about degree programs. Depending on your career field, you may have a handful of certifications you can add to your résumé. Those things don't just add letters after your name; they also give you the chance to learn new ways to do your job better. You could also collaborate with peers and share best practices as a group. As you open your eyes to how other people do the same job you're doing, you may be surprised to learn all the different strategies and techniques others have developed. Nothing gives you a new perspective on an old, familiar job better than hearing how someone else does it. Or—and you may not like this option—you could always pick up a second job. A part-time job in a different or related field gives you the chance to earn extra income while you learn new skills. If you're smart about it, a part-time job can be a training program that *pays you.*

Of course, it's not easy to invest time and effort into training programs or learning an entirely new method for doing a job you've already been doing for ten years. But that shouldn't stop you. Strive to be like the 94% of millionaires who aren't scared to try difficult things to get new results. If it's easy, it probably won't help much—so don't be afraid to challenge yourself. We found that 86% of millionaires believe challenging themselves will make them smarter. Remember, if the goal is to better yourself, that's going to require some effort.

Better Your Health

You can't build wealth if you can't work, and you can't work if your body is broken down from years of abuse and neglect. If you fuel your days with nothing but donuts and energy drinks, and if the only exercise you ever get is walking to and from the break room, then let me give you a word of advice: get off your butt! Millionaires prioritize their personal health. Eighty percent exercise three or more times a week, compared to 55% of the general population.[28] More than a third (35%) are basically health nuts, because they work out five or more days a week. Compare that to the more than one-third of Americans who are considered obese by the Center for Disease Control and Prevention.[29] Millionaire-minded people have things to do, and they refuse to let a sick, tired, old, broken, lazy body drag them down.

We already saw that 99% of millionaires are considered hard workers by their friends and family, and now we know that 80% work out at least three days a week. When do they find time to get everything done? They don't. Millionaires don't *find* time; they *make* time. And for most millionaires, that means getting up early in the morning. Seventy percent of them are considered early risers, compared to 44% of the general population. And they don't stay up too late either—only 30% consider themselves to be night owls. They get the rest they need to charge themselves up for a busy day. By not staying up too late, getting up early, and prioritizing their health, millionaires have the physical strength, stamina, and mental clarity they need to power through each day's goals.

Better Your Kids

It's clear the average millionaire lives a disciplined life of saving, investing, avoiding debt, setting goals, and working hard. But what about their adult children? Are today's millionaires guilty of creating a new generation of trust-fund babies and perpetual basement dwellers? No way. Only 6% of millionaires give monthly support to their children over the age of twenty-five, and only 18% do so on a periodic basis. And, while this may freak out many helicopter parents, 71% of millionaires *never* give financial support to their children over the age of twenty-five. Not only do millionaires refuse to financially support their grown children, but they also don't give them a free place to live. Only 8% of millionaires say their adult children live with them. The other 92% are happy to let the little birdies leave the nest and take care of themselves.

Forty Years of Hard Work

Millionaires constantly work to better themselves. They don't settle for what they have and who they are *today*; instead, they work to increase their education and their skill set to build more for tomorrow. A great example of that is Phil, a millionaire we interviewed in our research.

EVERYDAY MILLIONAIRE ——————————————————————

Phil grew up in Missouri. Both of his parents were teachers, so education was a priority in the family. He remembers his parents as being thrifty with their finances, and he admits they were great when it came to money management. In fact, Phil learned most of what he knows about money from his folks. Work was a big deal for the family, too. As a boy, Phil spent his days working on a dairy farm and picking cotton to earn money for himself. He wasn't scared of hard work, but those early days taught him he didn't want to spend the rest of his life out in the field. So he pursued a degree in chemical engineering and, like most of the millionaires in our research, he made it all the way through school with no student loans. Phil had plans for his life, and those plans didn't include years of student loan debt payments. Looking back, Phil said, "There is no way I would have borrowed money to go to school." He made it work with what he had, graduated with a great education, and took a job as an engineer right out of college.

Phil liked his company and he enjoyed his job, but he pushed himself to do more. After eight years in his engineering position, the company moved him into management, where he continued to grow and prosper for the next twenty years. When he saw more opportunities in the company's IT area, he transitioned to that field and spent the last twelve years of his career there. Every step of the way, Phil was invested in learning, growing, and sharpening his existing skills as well as learning entirely new skills. He was focused on making the biggest impact in his career, taking care of his family, and achieving financial independence. In all, Phil spent forty years—his entire career—at that one company.

Because he had invested so much into one company, Phil retired with a huge pension. Over the years, he also heavily invested in a 401(k) and an IRA. Now retired, and with a net worth of nearly $4 million, he has a great perspective on what it took to hit the millionaire mark. The most important thing, he said, is to fund retirement accounts like the 401(k) and IRA—and to start early. Phil also said the budget was central to his finances all these years. And, of course, Phil said he stayed away from credit cards and other forms of debt throughout his entire life. He knew he'd never build wealth if he wasted his money on interest payments. "When you live for now and live with debt," he said, "you will never become a millionaire." It's also clear that his commitment to bettering himself in his career was crucial. He never stopped learning or growing, and he made an enormous investment in one company over forty years and six different cities. Now retired with millions in his accounts, he knows that investment paid off.

MAKE TODAY COUNT

No matter if you've been lazy or unmotivated in the past, you can do better. It may not be easy, but there are things you can do every single day to improve your work ethic. When you boost your work ethic and output, you immediately boost your wealth-building potential. Even if you don't see an instant increase in your salary or net worth, you're making an investment in yourself. Over time, that investment will reap huge rewards. Remember, 80% of net-worth millionaires believe it's possible for *anyone* to do what they've done—but it'll take hard work. If you want to take a step closer to that goal, then take a lesson from the millionaire playbook and make these three things a priority *this week*:

1. *Get up early.* Don't miss what might be your most productive hours of the day. Turn off the TV, shut down social media, get to bed at a reasonable hour, and set your alarm. Try getting up one hour earlier for a few weeks (without cutting your sleep short) and see what you can accomplish with that extra hour of productivity.
2. *Read a book.* Find a book, class, podcast, or online training that can make an immediate impact on how well you do your job. Get up every day with a goal to learn one new thing that you can apply to your work. That'll be three hundred sixty-five improvements per year!
3. *Get moving.* It blows me away how people will pamper a car but trash their own bodies. Listen, you get one—and only one—body for your entire life. Your body is a finely tuned machine, so don't fuel it with garbage and leave it parked on the couch all day. You don't have to run a marathon; a simple twenty-minute walk after lunch every day can make a huge difference. Just get up and do *something*.

If you attack every day this way, you'll be on the right track. Make sure you hit the ground running every morning, knowing what you want to accomplish and ready to get the job done. Set a precedent for each day: refuse to be denied, shut down any obstacles or excuses that come your way, and don't let anyone—I mean anyone—get you sidetracked. Someone may come along and try to outsmart or outperform you, but you can make sure that no one will *ever* outwork you!

Millionaires Do

- **Work hard.** *Nearly all—99% of millionaires—say their friends and family members would describe them as hard workers.*

- **Believe reaching millionaire status is more about how hard you work than how much you make.** *93% of millionaires say they got there by hard work rather than big salaries.*

- **Enjoy their jobs.** *96% of millionaires enjoyed what they did for a career, and 64% say they "loved" their jobs.*

- **Exercise regularly.** *80% of millionaires exercise three or more times a week, compared to 55% of the general population.*

- **Wake up early.** *70% of millionaires are considered early risers, compared to 44% of the general population.*

Millionaires Don't

- *All retire when they hit $1 million net worth.* Only 38% of them are fully retired.

- *Support their adult children.* Only 6% of millionaires give monthly support to their children over the age of twenty-five—and 71% of millionaires never do.

- *Allow their grown children to live with them.* Only 8% of millionaires say their adult children live at home with them.

The key is to start saving and investing early—and to live on less than you make. Compound interest will get you there over the long haul. No use trying to keep up with the Joneses. They're broke!

— ANNE, $1.4 MILLION NET WORTH

Chapter 10

Stick to It

Millionaires Are Consistent

"We are what we repeatedly do. Excellence, then, is not an act, but a habit."

That sounds like one of those down-home, old-school pieces of advice we've heard from many of the millionaires in our study, but it's not. That sentiment is a little older—*way older.* Author Will Durant summed up fourth-century wisdom from the great philosopher Aristotle in that one line, explaining that the secret to excellence is simply doing the same things over and over again. We have a word for that today: *consistency.* Consistency is the key that brings all these millionaire attributes together. You can take responsibility, you can be intentional, you can set goals, and you can work hard. But, if you don't do these things *repeatedly*—year after year, decade after decade—then you'll never get the results you want. Your millionaire goals won't crash and burn; they'll just fizzle and sputter out. It's like taking your foot off the gas while you're driving down the highway—your car won't blow up, but it will gradually coast to a complete stop. All the progress you've made up to that point won't matter, because you'll be sitting on the side of the road. You would have lost all your momentum, and once that happens, you may never get it back.

KEEP YOUR MOMENTUM

Too often we act like consistency is a bad thing. We whine about being bored with the same thing all the time. We excuse our stupid decisions because "variety is the spice of life." Listen, variety may spice up your social life, but it'll spoil your financial life. It's easy to ignore the powerful force of consistency because it often fades into the background. However, consistency builds momentum. And we like consistency. We like not having to map out and meticulously plan our daily drive to work. We like being around and trusting the same people we've known for twenty years. We like having our paychecks hit our bank accounts like clockwork twice a month. We like being able to count on our coworkers who have proven themselves in the past. You know what we don't like? When things get out of whack. When we expect one thing and get another. When "variety" pops up and slows down the momentum we've been building. Consistency may feel boring sometimes, but when something's working, why would you want to switch gears?

Patience Pays Off

Millionaires don't change their plan midstream if it's working for them, and they don't stop halfway to the goal. As we saw earlier, our research found that 98% of millionaires finish what they start; they don't leave things undone. That's because becoming a net-worth millionaire is more than a thought or hope. It goes beyond simply saying, "I'd like to" or "I wish I could." If you want to become one of America's millionaires, you've got to commit yourself to the long, hard work of getting there. You've got to commit to it deep in the very core of your being, and it needs to guide your decisions and your actions for the next ten, twenty, or thirty years. You need to attack this goal the way Herb and Joan did, a millionaire couple from South Carolina.

EVERYDAY MILLIONAIRES

Herb and Joan are the picture of consistency, and their early retirement proves it. Herb grew up in a traditional middle-class family, and his father was intentional about teaching him how to work and save. As a boy, Herb sold bags of peanuts for a dime, and his dad showed him how to allocate part of his money to savings and part to spending. His dad often said, "Always give some money to your future. Don't give it all to your present." That simple lesson guided Herb's finances his entire life.

Herb earned his business administration degree at The Citadel and then took a job at a large phone company. He stayed with that company for thirty years—which is something we don't often see anymore. During that time, Herb and Joan had a goal of financial independence. They had a clear picture of what life would look like when they weren't dependent on a full-time job for their income, and they talked about that goal often. To get there, they both maxed out their 401(k) plans and added in some other stock market investments. Herb said the 401(k) with his company's matching dollars was the easiest way to hit his millionaire goal, even though it took a few decades to do it.

At age fifty-two, the couple was able to declare their financial independence in the best way possible. After thirty years with the phone company, Herb realized his job wasn't fun anymore. That's just a fact of life for most working Americans. Too many people get up every morning and drive to a job they hate because they can't afford to lose the income. Not Herb. When he realized he wasn't having any fun, he checked his investments, saw that he and Joan had plenty of money to live on for the rest of their lives, and left his job. He took early retirement at fifty-two—*because he could afford to*. He and Joan were millionaires by then, and millionaires get to make those kinds of decisions.

Looking back, the couple says their financial success comes down to four key factors. First, they said it took a commitment to a long-term goal. They knew from the start that it wouldn't happen fast, but they knew it would happen eventually. Second, they said it required discipline. They had opportunities to derail their plan every day, and they needed discipline to stay on track. Third, they said their agreement as a couple was absolutely vital. We'll talk more about that in a minute. Fourth, the couple knew from the outset that their plan would require patience. They knew it would take a while to get where they wanted to be, but today—retired in their fifties and with a net worth of $2.9 million—they know it was worth it.

When we asked them why they thought most people fail to become millionaires, they didn't hesitate. Herb said it comes down to a lack of planning and self-control, two things he learned in spades during his military training at The Citadel. "Trying to become a millionaire by playing the lottery is a stupid plan," he said. "Investing may not be sexy, but it is the best way to grow wealth."

Better Together

Herb and Joan's story highlights something important that we don't want to miss: their goal was to get to the millionaire finish line *together*. A broken marriage would have been a failure for them no matter what their finances looked like at retirement. This points to something we noted in a shocking majority of millionaires: strong, healthy, long-lasting marriages. We found that 80% of millionaires are married, compared to 49% of the general population.

More significantly, 63% of millionaires are in a first marriage, compared to only 38% of the general population. Finally, only 5% of millionaires report being currently divorced, compared to 19% of the general population. So, the general population has *four times* the divorce rate than that of millionaires!

These successful millionaires demonstrate consistency not just in their finances, but also in their marriages and relationships, as 75% of married millionaires have been married for thirty-two years on average. This means most of these couples built their wealth, year after year, together. The result of working side by side for so long toward a common goal is apparently important for marriage, too, as an overwhelming 91% of millionaires say their marriage is either good or great. And if you're wondering where they learned this, the answer probably won't surprise you: their own parents. Our research revealed that 88% of millionaires come from families with parents who stayed married, compared to 72% of the general population. Let's flip that around and see it the other way. We're saying that 12% of millionaires had divorced parents, compared to 28% of the general population. That means a child from a committed, *consistent* household is more than twice as likely to become a millionaire.

80% of millionaires are married, compared to **49%** of the general population.

These numbers demonstrate something I've learned from all the millionaires I've known, talked to, and worked with. A millionaire mind-set isn't just about money. The money is important, but it's not the *most important* thing—not by a long shot. A successful life is about character, commitment, responsibility, intentionality, hard work, and goal setting in every part of life. These people don't want to be successful *only* in their finances. They want to have successful marriages and friendships. They want to be successful at work, knowing they're making a difference in the world. Simply put, they want to be successful in their *lives*. That's the power of consistency. They get a picture in their minds of what they want their lives— their whole lives—to look like, and they do whatever it takes to accomplish that vision.

CONSISTENCY REQUIRES PATIENCE AND PASSION

It should be clear by now that consistency doesn't just *happen* on its own—in any part of your life but *especially* your finances. Consistency requires planning, preparation, patience, and passion. Patience and passion are extremely important here because those are the things that will keep you committed to your long-term goals for the long haul. If you have passion, then you'll find more ways to get the job done. As you see something working, you'll get more excited and more invested, and you will go out of your way to find more ways to speed up the process. You have to keep the "speeding up" part in perspective, though. Patience gives you the long-term view you need to stay focused through the years, to keep you from getting distracted by all the stupid things everyone around you is wasting their money on. Like I said before, becoming a millionaire can't simply be an idea, a hope, or a dream; it has to become a way of life, something that drives your decisions for decades.

Opportunity Cost Is Opportunity Lost

I've said before that 79% of millionaires used their company-sponsored retirement plans to reach the millionaire mark, making it the number one vehicle for wealth building. What we also learned is that 75% of millionaires make regular, consistent investing part of their ongoing personal finances. That means these people have chosen to say no to whatever flashy thing screams for their attention on any given day, and they've remained focused on their ongoing march toward financial independence. They, like Herb earlier in this chapter, have chosen to give their money to the future instead of giving it all to the present. That's what adults do; they can choose to say no to impulse for the sake of longer-term goals. Children do the opposite. Children are slaves to their desire, only focusing on the fun they can have *today*. We all have that battle raging within; we each have an adult and a child inside of us, but we can't let the child make our financial decisions. Kids aren't consistent—they're impulsive. When you throw your investing strategy out the window just to buy a new car or choose to spend this month's investing dollars on a new TV instead, you're acting like a child. And if that goes on too long, you'll hit retirement having only what children have: big dreams and empty pockets.

Make Money While You Sleep

You need to approach retirement the way Gary, a retired educator from Iowa, did.

EVERYDAY MILLIONAIRES ————————————————————

Gary and his wife, Susan, have done an incredible job amassing a net worth far above the $1 million mark—but it didn't happen overnight. Gary grew up dirt poor. His parents were still teenagers when Gary was born, and his father worked several different farm jobs during Gary's early childhood. They eventually moved onto a rental farm when he was six years old, and his parents put him to work immediately. By age nine, he was working full time on the farm when he wasn't in school. The family never had any money. They had eggs every day for breakfast

193

and lunch from the chickens on the farm, and Gary even remembers his mother cooking up a pot of weeds from the garden one night when a drought had knocked out their vegetables. Despite these rough times, the family stuck together and made it work. Even today, Gary looks back on his parents as two of his greatest millionaire influences.

He and Susan married at age nineteen, and Gary attended a local college—a first for his family. Afterward, he took a teaching position and the couple started a family. Raising kids put a spotlight on his low teaching salary, though. It dawned on him that he couldn't even afford to save up for his children's college education, so he started looking for ways to boost his income. Ultimately, Gary decided to return to school and get a master's degree, which would increase his teacher's pay. "If you're going to be there teaching the same number of hours," he said, "you might as well get the most money you can per hour." Susan also added to the family income by going to school for an education degree and becoming a teacher herself. In all, Gary spent twenty years teaching, followed by another nine years in school administration. Then, after his retirement, he spent another five years teaching part time at a nearby college.

Throughout his and Susan's careers, the couple saved consistently month after month. They lived frugally and weren't afraid to make short-term sacrifices for long-term gains. Gary believes the main thing that keeps people from becoming millionaires is failing to understand what they could do with just a little bit of sacrifice. In fact, this couple didn't even buy their first home until they had saved up enough to pay cash, something that took a while on their teacher salaries. Over several decades, they took advantage of the available pensions and invested regularly into an IRA. They also set goals throughout their marriage to buy tracts of ranch land as an investment. Their first goal was to purchase 320 acres of grass. When they hit that goal, they set a new one. When they hit the new goal, they did it again. And again. And again. Today, Gary and Susan own 5,400 acres of land in Iowa, which they rent out to farmers. That not only provides a steady stream of passive rental income but also, along with their other investments, contributes to their incredible $10 million net worth today. Gary set those goals based on these wise words from his father: "You'll never get ahead unless you find a way to make money while you're sleeping."

Making money while you're asleep is one of the key strategies millionaires use to build wealth, but that only happens when you make a plan and work toward it consistently over time. So let's dig in to better understand how these men and women wake up wealthier than they were when they went to bed. It starts by understanding compound interest.

Understanding Compound Interest

Albert Einstein is thought to have said, "Compound interest is the eighth wonder of the world. He who understands it *earns* it. He who doesn't *pays* it. Compound interest is the most powerful force in the universe." What makes compound interest so unbelievably powerful? Time. Investing early and consistently over a long period of time allows you to take advantage of the two most powerful forces in all of finance: time and compound interest. When you put money into an investment and let it sit awhile, your money grows from the interest you earn. If you put $1,000 in originally, you might have $1,100 a year later. That extra $100 is the result of the interest you earned. What happens in the second year? Well, now you aren't earning interest on $1,000; you're earning interest on $1,100. So the money that grew from interest in the first year is now earning interest itself. That's what *compounding* means—it's when your interest earns interest. Your money is basically creating *more* money, and it keeps doing that on its own—morning, noon, and night.

The effect that time and compound interest have on your money is mind-blowing. Let me put it into perspective for you. What if I offered you a choice: you can have $1 million cash *right now* and walk away, or you can have one penny right now. If you choose the penny, you can come back tomorrow, and I'll double it, leaving you with two pennies. Then I'll double it again the next day, bringing your grand total to four cents after three days. I'll keep doubling it every day for a month—thirty-one days in all. Which of these two choices sounds like the better deal? Most people would take the $1 million and run away laughing. Who would choose pennies over a cool million? Here's the thing, though: those pennies keep on doubling. After a week, you'd have $1.27, which doesn't sound great. After two weeks, you'd be up to $163.83. After three weeks, things would start to get interesting: your $163.83 would have jumped up to $20,971.51. One week later, at day twenty-eight, you'd be up to $2,684,354.55. You're a multimillionaire! But get this: three days later, at the end of the month, the penny you started with would now be worth $21,474,836.47! You'd have more than $21 million—twenty-one times what you would have if you had chosen the $1 million on day one—and the only thing it cost you was a little time.

Sure, this is an exaggerated example. You're not going to find any investment that doubles your money every day forever. However, this illustration does show the unbelievable power of time and compound interest on your money. The point here is that people too often make decisions with a short-term view. They're too quick to choose the immediate thrill over the long-term goal. Remember, that's what children do. That's the kind of shortsighted thinking that will keep you living paycheck to paycheck for the rest of your life. I want you to start looking beyond the short-term and get comfortable as you work toward the bigger, better reward that is still years ahead of you. That's how millionaires like Gary and Susan built their wealth. They didn't hesitate to put their short-term wants on hold to maximize their long-term reward. Looking back, Gary says, "If someone had told me where we would be today when we were only making $6,300 per year teaching, I wouldn't have believed it." However, by consistently saving and sacrificing, and by taking advantage of the power of time, Gary and Susan aren't *just* millionaires—they're *multimillionaires*. They stuck to it and got the job *done*.

CONSISTENT INVESTING

Compound interest works, but it won't make you a millionaire overnight. It took years—decades—of hard work, sacrifice, and consistent investing before the average millionaire hit the mark. But that's okay with them; they have time. So, by this point, you're probably wondering what they're investing in—and how you can do the same. If millionaires avoid risky investments, as we've seen at length, then what are the safe, proven financial vehicles they use to build wealth? Believe it or not, it all comes down to the 401(k) or the company plan.

The Company Plan Is Crucial

We know that the employer-sponsored retirement plan is the number one way the millionaires we studied built their wealth. So, if I know that the majority of millionaires built their net worth this way and would advise me to do the same, I think that's probably something I should think about, don't you? Why would I reinvent the wheel if there's already a proven plan for building wealth that has worked for the vast majority of millionaires in this country?

Despite how dumb that sounds, it's shocking how many people *aren't* taking this advice from the nation's millionaires. Bankrate reports that only one in three millennials invest in the stock market, including company-sponsored plans.[30] Why not? Half of them say the fear of losing money is too great an obstacle.[31] What they don't realize is that they are *already* losing money by not taking advantage of these company plans. If you're young, at this point you may be doubting your ability to invest. But no matter your income or the cost of living in your area, once you're debt-free, you need to make a way to put money into your retirement plan—whatever it takes. If you're new in the workforce, you should just now be starting what will be a long career. By not investing during these critical first few years in a new job, you're robbing yourself of the power of time. And time, as you know, is the engine that drives your wealth-building investments. Delaying investing just ten years can make a massive difference in your net worth at retirement. If you're reading this in your twenties and haven't jumped into your company's 401(k) yet and you're debt-free, do it *today*.

Don't tell me you can't afford it, either. If I could afford it when I was just starting out, I know you can. In my first job as an assistant coach at California University of Pennsylvania, I made a whopping $13,000 salary. I was rich! Okay, not really. Even in the early 1990s, $13,000 wasn't much money. It was hard to get by on just over $1,000 a month, but I made it work. Six months into my position, my boss, the head coach, told me I was eligible to participate in the school's 403(b) program. At the time, I had no idea what that meant. He said, "That's a retirement savings program that lets you save for the future with some tax benefits. You need to do this, and you need to do it right now." I told him no thanks. At twenty-one years old, I was barely making any money, and I wasn't that concerned with retirement yet. Well, that old coach *made* me get concerned. He sat me down, put the enrollment form in front of me, and argued with me until I finally signed the form just to get out of there. When I left his office, he said, "Chris, you'll thank me for this." Now, as I look back twenty-five years later, I really can thank him. He taught me at a critical age that saving for the future was important. He showed me that it didn't matter how much or how little money I made; I could always afford to set some aside for wealth building—and so can you.

How to Invest

Financial experts—myself included—recommend investing 15% of your income into retirement savings throughout your working life. That's enough to get your wealth building off to a great start, but not so much that it'll get in the way of paying off your house. These are two goals that will take years to accomplish, so make sure you're giving each one the proper time, attention, and cash flow it deserves. Now, what do you do with that 15%? I want to walk you through a simple, three-step plan for making the most of your contributions. This includes investing money both inside and outside company-sponsored plans, which is what millionaires do. We've seen that 79% of millionaires invest in a company retirement plan, but we also found that 74% invest *outside* of a company plan. That means most of these men and women invest in *both*, and I can show you the best way. Do these things in this order, and you'll be on your way toward financial independence.

79% of millionaires invest *inside* a company plan and **74%** invest *outside* a company plan, meaning most of them invest in *both*.

First, if your company offers a match on your 401(k), you should invest in your 401(k) *up to the match*. So, if your company matches 4%, you'll contribute 4% of your income there to take advantage of that free money. If your company offers a Roth 401(k) option, that's the one to go with. I'll explain the ins and outs of the 401(k) below. For now, just know that the 401(k) match is your starting point.

Second, above the 401(k) match, you'll move to a Roth IRA. A Roth IRA is an amazing retirement option that enables your money to grow *tax-free*. You'd set this up on your own, separately from the 401(k), so talk to an investment professional for help. This is also where you'd *start* investing if your company does not offer a 401(k) match. The Roth IRA works pretty much the same way as a Roth 401(k). The main difference is that an IRA gives you more fund options to choose from than what your company offers inside their 401(k) plan. There's a maximum contribution limit for Roth IRAs ($5,500 per person under age fifty as of 2018). If you're married filing jointly, though, both spouses can have a Roth IRA—even if one doesn't work. So, each spouse could max out a Roth IRA in their name up to $5,500 each, or $11,000 total (as of 2018). After matching the 401(k) and putting up to $11,000 into a Roth IRA, most couples hit their 15% contribution goal right here.

Third, if you max out the Roth IRA and *still* haven't hit 15% of your income in contributions, then go back to the 401(k) and finish your 15% there. One quick note on income, though. You can't open a Roth IRA if your income is too high ($135,000 individually or $199,000 for married couples filing jointly as of 2018). If that excludes you, then you'd just invest your full 15% into the 401(k) and be done with it.

Make the Most of Your 401(k) or Company Plan

Since the company retirement plan is the most common way millionaires build wealth, let's break down how to use it to get the biggest bang for your investing buck. These rules generally apply to the 401(k) as well as other company-sponsored plans, such as the 403(b) you might have in a medical or nonprofit profession.

First, sign up for your 401(k) plan's automated paycheck withdrawals. Company-sponsored retirement plans like the 401(k) make it easy to contribute, because the investment comes right out of your paycheck. You never bring the money home, so you don't feel like it's missing. It happens automatically behind the scenes, so you can set it and forget it. In fact, 91% of 401(k) investors report the payroll deduction makes it easier for them to save.[32] This is especially powerful if you're able to participate in a 401(k) immediately when you start a new job. Just set up your contribution to start with your first paycheck, and you'll never miss it—even though it'll be automatically building your future millions one paycheck at a time.

Second, if your company offers a Roth 401(k) option, you should take it. The Roth 401(k) allows your money to grow *tax-free*, which should be your favorite phrase. It costs a little more on the front end because your Roth 401(k) investment uses after-tax dollars. The tradeoff, though, is that you won't pay a penny in taxes when you pull the money out at retirement. So basically, you're paying taxes on $100 today to avoid paying taxes on $1 million later. That's a good deal. This one option could literally save you hundreds of thousands of dollars in retirement, so don't miss it. When you see the word *Roth*, just say yes.

Third, if your company offers a 401(k) match, take it. I don't want to hear any excuses about this one. Think about it: your employer is actually offering you free money. If you make $50,000 a year and your company offers a 4% match, that's an extra $2,000 per year you could put toward wealth building. Why on earth would you not take that? That $2,000 per year *alone* could almost make you a millionaire! Say you start a job at age twenty-five making $50,000 per year and the company offers a 4% 401(k) match. Now, of course you're going to invest 15% of your income, because that's what smart people do. But just for the fun of it, let's only look at the 4% match amount and see what happens. A 4% match on a $50,000 salary means you're putting in $2,000 a year and the company is matching $2,000 a year, giving you $4,000 a year total going into your 401(k). If that's all you ever do, you'd retire at age sixty-five with almost $2 million—and *half* of that would be from the free money your company gave you! Don't be stupid. If your company wants to give you $1 million, take it.

You should still take advantage of the 401(k) even if your company doesn't offer a match—assuming you've already maxed out your Roth IRA like we discussed above. Even without matching funds, your company is providing a way for you to maximize your investing dollars through the 401(k) because of how taxes are treated. Eighty percent of 401(k) investors say the tax treatment alone—totally separate from any match—is a huge incentive for investing.[33] If you invest in a regular (non-Roth) 401(k), the money you put into it doesn't have any taxes taken out. So, if you put $100 into your 401(k) in one pay period, the *whole* $100 goes into the investment. If you bring the money home first, though, that $100 becomes more like $75 after taxes. By bringing it home, you've given yourself less to work with. Think of it this way: even if your employer doesn't offer a match, you're still getting the *effect* of a match by avoiding taxes on your contributions. You're being smart with your money by putting your education and experience to work for you. Now you're thinking like a millionaire.

While 15% should be your *starting point* for your investing, it's not all you should *ever* do. Remember, the reason we start with only 15% is because you still need some extra income to throw at your mortgage. Once you finally pay your house off, though, you can fire all your cannons at your 401(k). That's when you can really go for it, taking your contributions up to the maximum amount allowed. The federal limit changes every year, so you want to keep an eye on that. For 2018, for example, it's $18,500 per employee (not including employer matching). Once you're over age fifty, you can take advantage of 401(k) catch-up contributions, which allow you to invest even more above the federal limit. The catch-up max for 2018 is $6,000, but again, it changes all the time. Talk to your investment professional or your company's 401(k) representative to get the current guidelines.

Track Your Investments

While the 401(k) gives you an easy way to invest, you don't want to mentally check out of the whole process. Your 401(k) provider will keep you informed at least once a quarter of how your investments are doing. That quarterly update is your 401(k) statement, and it shows the state of your account just like your monthly bank statement does. Do not—and I repeat, *do not*—throw this statement away without looking at it. This report shows you what kind of progress you're making toward your millionaire goals. It's a scorecard that tells you whether or not your investments are working for you. Plus, as you get used to investing, it helps you identify market trends. You may see all kinds of financial ups and downs in the news, but these things take on new life when you see them show up on your personal investing statement. You may find out that half of what you see on TV is a lie. Or you may find out that current events really do impact your life on a direct, intimate level. All this works to turn you into a seasoned, well-informed investor—and that's what you want to be.

Of course, I need to throw in a warning here. There will be times when you open your statement and see that you actually *lost* money in a quarter. It stinks, but this is *going* to happen. Get ready for it. It's easy to look at your statement for one quarter and freak out if the market's down. I've seen people overreact in crazy ways, from cashing out their 401(k) to moving all their investments around on a whim. Don't do it! There will always be ups and downs in the stock market. Like anything else with investing, you need to focus on the long-term plan, not the short-term hiccup. So, when your statement comes, you need to open it, make sure everything is accurate, and take a minute to reaffirm what you're doing and why you're doing it. Then, whether the report has good news or bad news, fold it up and file it away. Like I often say, the market is like a roller coaster. It's a wild ride sometimes, but the only way you'll get hurt is if you jump off.

Get Professional Help

Ally Financial reports that 61% of all working adults say investing in the market is "scary or intimidating."[34] Well, let me tell you something scary and intimidating: if you let fear prevent you from participating in your best wealth-building years, you're going to retire broke, ashamed, stressed out, and looking to others to take care of you. Millionaires don't let fear stop them from achieving their goals, and they don't let intimidation scare them off from focusing on something over several years and decades.

That may be because they weren't too scared to ask for help. As we've seen in other chapters, 98% of millionaires integrated feedback from others into their financial behaviors and 68% worked with a financial planner to achieve their net worth. I understand that investing can be scary. If you don't know what you're doing and you aren't familiar with all the options, *anything* can look too risky. But seriously, don't let fear get in the way of achieving your millionaire goals. Remember, you *can* do this. Find a qualified professional who will spend time with you, get to know you and your unique situation, and make solid recommendations on how to maximize your 401(k) and other investment options. This is someone who is up to date on recent market trends and forecasts, so they should be able to teach you how the market works and give you some great advice. I like the way Herb, the millionaire we met earlier in this chapter, put it: "I'm not a heart surgeon, so I use a professional when I need surgery. I'm not a dentist, so I go to a professional when I need dental work. And, I'm not a professional investor, so I depend on a professional financial advisor to guide me."

If you don't know how or where to find someone, I can help. I have a network of recommended, intelligent, well-qualified investing pros all over the country. These men and women will spend time teaching you how to make the best decisions for your money. Check out my site, www.chrishogan360.com, to get connected with someone near you. When you meet with a pro, though, never forget that *you're* in charge. Your investment professional's job is to teach you how these things work so you can make your own decisions. If you ever sit down with someone who just wants to tell you what to do with your money, run. To build wealth, you need to prove that you're responsible for your own financial decisions. Never hand off that responsibility to someone else—including your investment professional. It's your money, so you've got to own your own decisions with it. Remember what we saw earlier: 84% of millionaires say achieving a high net worth is about smart habits and *things they can control*. You can't control anything if you let other people make all your decisions.

BE DISCIPLINED AND STICK WITH IT

Time and consistency can move mountains—*literally*. If you give a little stream of moving water enough time, it can cut a mountain in half. Most people never apply that principle to their finances, though. They don't believe building wealth simply comes down to having the discipline to set goals, start early, and work toward them day after day, year after year, and decade after decade. As we wrap up this discussion on the power of consistency, I can't think of a better example than Tori, a millionaire we talked to from Indiana.

EVERYDAY MILLIONAIRE

Tori grew up in a lower-middle-class family and was responsible for her own finances at a young age. She never got an allowance and always had to work for every dollar she had. Well, almost every dollar. She remembers her aunt giving her a birthday card for her seventh birthday. When she opened the card, Tori found ten dimes taped to the inside. It was such a special, significant gift that Tori never spent the money. In fact, she still has that card—dimes included—as one of her most prized possessions.

All through high school, Tori had a specific career goal: she wanted to be a CPA. Back then, she says, women weren't generally working as CPAs. She didn't let that stop her, though. She completed her degree and started working in accounting right out of college. Her family's financial background and her accounting education shaped her approach to money. Because of the money stress she constantly saw in her parents, Tori committed early on that she would become financially independent. From the day she became responsible for her own finances at age fifteen, she set a goal of having enough money to live comfortably—more comfortably than her parents could have imagined. Throughout her entire career, Tori kept that goal in mind, and it guided all her financial decisions. She never bought anything she couldn't pay cash for. She worked and saved to put herself through school and to purchase her own home. When her friends bought brand-new cars, she bought five-year-old cars. She never got distracted, and she never stopped saving. Today, she and her husband are retired multimillionaires with a net worth of $2.7 million and are living the life they've dreamed of—and worked for—for decades.

Tori knows she's lived a much different life than most people. As an accountant, she's seen people waste an unbelievable amount of money. She's seen every mistake imaginable, watching families lose millions in potential wealth by running after new cars, giant houses, and ridiculous vacations. When we asked Tori what her secret was, though, she said everything she's accomplished is the result of starting early, sticking with it, and the power of compound interest. She knows, even now in retirement, that the decisions she made in her twenties led her directly to where she is today. Her advice to the next generation? It's simple, she says. "Be disciplined early on and stick to it for at least ten years." She's learned through decades of patience and hard work that consistency pays off . . . *big time.*

Be disciplined early on and stick to it. Such a simple formula, but it captures everything I've been talking about. Slow and steady, low and slow, you will build wealth if you do what these millionaires have done: consistently invest in your 401(k) or other retirement accounts, consistently increase your contributions, and consistently leave it alone. I know it won't happen overnight; it didn't for any of the millionaires we talked to. But at the end of the day, it *will* happen.

Millionaires Do ────────────────────

- **Stay married.** *63% of millionaires are in a first marriage, and 75% of married millionaires have been married for thirty-two years on average.*

- **Take advantage of their company retirement plans.** *79% of millionaires used their company-sponsored plan to reach millionaire status.*

- **Invest consistently.** *75% make regular, consistent investing part of their ongoing personal finances.*

- **Invest in other ways.** *While 79% of millionaires invest inside a company plan, 74% invest outside a company plan, meaning most of them do both.*

Millionaires Don't

- *Have miserable marriages.* 91% of millionaires say their marriage is either good or great.

- *Have sophisticated or complicated retirement plans and investment strategies.* The company-sponsored retirement plan is the number one way these millionaires built their wealth.

- *Solely rely on themselves for investment planning.* 68% worked with an investment professional to achieve their net worth.

My wife and I are pretty simple. Very few people in our circle would believe we have over a million dollars, much less 8.7 million dollars. We bought a home for our daughter and her husband and gifted money to two nephews to help them buy homes. Our passion is helping others with education expenses. Being able to give is so much more rewarding than wishing you were able to give!

—JOHN, $8.7 MILLION NET WORTH

Chapter 11

The Decision Is Up to You

Ten thousand millionaires. We talked to 10,000 millionaires about what wealth really looks like in America today, and you may have been surprised by what we found. We saw that there are more millionaires in the country today than ever before—almost eleven million of them.[35] We learned who they are, how they act, and how they built wealth. We saw what their lives looked like before, during, and after their wealth building. We've seen where they came from—and where their *wealth* came from. We didn't just look at the stats; we got to know these people. We examined story after story of America's millionaires. And, like I told you early in the book, most of these stories are a little boring. These men and women didn't have crazy, bold, unusual, world-changing careers. They're teachers and accountants. Military personnel and mid-level management. Engineers and farmers. Remember, only 15% of millionaires held senior leadership positions in their careers; the rest—a whopping 85%—were regular people working regular jobs. And now they're millionaires.

In the first part of the book, we debunked three myth categories about the typical millionaire. We saw that what most people assume about millionaires is just plain wrong—nothing more than prejudice, lies, and excuses. First, we tore apart the myth that wealthy people didn't earn or deserve their wealth. There were no enormous inheritances or luck involved. Second, we examined the myth that says wealthy people take crazy risks with their money, either with risky investments or stupid, get-rich-quick schemes. The research showed us that the millionaires in our study all built their wealth slowly and steadily with commonly available retirement accounts like the 401(k). Third, we answered the myth that wealthy people have a leg up in their education or careers. Rather than any unfair advantages, we found that the typical millionaire has a public or state school degree and a normal job with a normal salary. These myths are often used by people to excuse a lack of effort, to rationalize why they aren't winning with money. But these excuses don't hold any water. And now you know the truth: you can do better—no matter your background, income, or education—and, ultimately, you are the one with the power to accomplish your money goals.

Then we dug in our heels and examined five key character traits of the typical American millionaire. Television likes to portray these men and women as sleazy, dishonest, unreliable, narcissistic monsters, but we know better. We saw that the average millionaires in America take responsibility for themselves, their wealth, and their needs; they're intentional about what they're doing and where they want their lives to go; they set goals and keep those goals front and center until they achieve them; they work their butts off and know the dignity and honor in a good day's labor; and they stay consistent in the day-to-day, slow-and-steady progress toward their long-term goals. You may have had your doubts about millionaires and their character before, but now you know the reality. These aren't flashy, big-headed morons doing everything they can to show off their wealth; they're simple, humble, happy people who you'd never know were millionaires. Every single one of them earned and deserved their wealth, and they're using it responsibly, being blessings to their families and communities. So, please, let's stop portraying these hardworking Americans as stuffy, high-brow losers, living lavish lifestyles, okay? The research shows that's simply not true.

Now that you know who these everyday millionaires are, how they act, and how they smashed their wealth-building goals, let's tackle one more key issue. We've spent this entire book talking about, dreaming about, and working toward financial independence. We've seen how others have done it, what they look like, and how they act. It's time to turn the tables a little bit. We know what financial independence looks like for *them*. Now I want you to get a vision for what it would look like for *you*.

UNDERSTANDING FINANCIAL INDEPENDENCE

In its truest sense, financial independence means freedom. No, I'm not talking about some vague notion of *financial freedom*. I don't believe anyone is ever free from their finances. You'll always have to spend time and attention on your finances, whether they're good or bad. Your money is yours to manage, and it's impossible to manage anything that you don't stay connected to often. We've seen that millionaires never outgrow the act of budgeting or setting financial goals, so stop thinking about financial independence as some point in the future when you don't have to think about money anymore. Get over it. You'll *always* have to think about money. The goal is to make those thoughts and conversations exciting and fun! Freedom is powerful, and it can change your life—if you understand the proper context. So, what is the freedom I'm talking about? I can break it down into three parts: debt, assets, and income.

The Freedom of Financial Independence

First, financial independence means you're free from debt. I mean *totally* free, house and all. At this point, you don't owe anything to anyone. Everything you have is *yours*, and it all goes in your asset column. Your liability column is completely empty. There are no credit card bills, car loans, mortgage payments, or student loans (yours or your kids'). There is no risk of default, no creditors barking for your money, and not a single dime wasted on interest payments. Your money is, once and for all, free from all other claims.

Second, financial independence means your assets have grown into a mountain of wealth. We've seen how investing even a small amount consistently can make you a multimillionaire by retirement. If you get a $50,000 job right out of college and invest the recommended 15% of your income into your 401(k), you could retire with more than $3.6 million by age sixty-five. And guess what? That happens even if you never get a raise, never get an inheritance, and never win the lottery. If you want to see something really crazy, dig into the math in this example. Forty years of saving 15% of $50,000 means you're investing $625 per month. After forty years, your all-time contributions would total $300,000. Don't miss that. You would have only put in $300,000, but you'd end up with $3.6 million. By starting early, staying consistent, and putting your money to work month after month, you would have literally *created* more than $3 million in wealth. That is free money, and it is yours for the taking. Do you think you'd be financially independent if you were debt-free, had a paid-for home, and had $3.6 million sitting in the bank? Yeah, I do too.

Third, financial independence means you have a self-sustaining income stream for the rest of your life. Here, your investments have replaced your income. That's what we call the *pinnacle point*—when the income your investments create every year is more than the income you used to make at your job. Go back to the example above. If that was you, you lived on a $50,000 income throughout your entire working life. Then, when it was time to retire, you started living off your investments. Even if you lived on a conservative 4% of your total $3.6 million nest egg, you'd have a retirement income of $144,000 per year. Your investments would pay you almost three times what your full-time job paid you! That's true financial independence, because that income happens automatically. You don't have to work for it. It rolls in no matter where you are—whether you're at work, volunteering, traveling the world, or playing golf. You can do whatever you want for the rest of your life without worrying about money.

And listen, I know I've been referring to retirement a lot, but financial independence doesn't have to wait until your sixties. Financial independence isn't an age; it's just math. Whenever you hit your financial milestones and have investment income that will support your lifestyle, you're financially independent. It doesn't matter if you're thirty-five or sixty-five. I've known people who busted it for the first twenty years of their career, and then retired in their early forties. If that's your goal, go for it.

Okay, let's break all this down. Financial independence means you've got no debt (including a paid-off home), your income comes from your assets instead of a paycheck, you've hit some key milestones, and you're experiencing freedom like you've never known. That sounds awesome, doesn't it? Even if you maintain a simple, frugal lifestyle at this point, can you imagine what it would feel like to know you had enough money to live on for the rest of your life without having to work? Cliff, a millionaire from Minnesota, knows what that's like. This guy has seen a dramatic swing in his net worth throughout his life.

EVERYDAY MILLIONAIRE ——————————————————————

Cliff came from a huge family—he's the oldest of ten children—and he remembers money always being tight as a kid. He said they always had food on the table, but there was never any extra money. That meant he was on his own when it came time for college. He worked his tail off to put himself through school, and he ultimately graduated with a double major. Cliff got a great job with an oil company right out of college, and he impressed his bosses and coworkers with his intelligence and stamina for long, hard days of work. The company promoted him every few years, and he eventually retired from there as the vice president in charge of global purchasing.

Throughout his career, Cliff and his amazing wife of fifty-eight years prioritized saving. He was used to living on little, and he never let his promotions or rising salary go to his head. Each raise meant more money to save. Sure, they enjoyed their life and never lacked anything they really wanted, but they were never interested in spending for the sake of spending. He taught himself the basics of investing early in his career and put systems in place for regular savings. Starting early, he said, was one of the big reasons for his wealth today. He invested whatever he could every step of his career, and he watched his investment portfolio grow year after year.

Cliff admits that he fell for some debt traps early in his adult life, but those days are far behind him. When we asked what advice he'd give future millionaires, he broke it down into two easy steps: "Get debt-free as soon as possible and have a plan for investing to be able to achieve what you want to do." For Cliff, "what you want to do" means being able to do *what* he wants *when* he wants. That's freedom in action. He and his wife, now worth $6.7 million, are enjoying an active life of traveling, fishing, and golf. That may not be *your* retirement dream, but it's theirs—and they did whatever it took to make that dream happen.

Financial Independence vs. Financial Dependence

Whenever I hear someone say they want to be rich, I know what they're *really* saying is that they want all the things wealth enables you to do. Like I've said, financial independence means freedom, and freedom is something we all want. When it comes to financial independence, I think we're basically talking about four things:

1. *Flexibility.* This comes down to freedom of time. You're not punching a time clock, and no boss is looking over your shoulder. This is where your calendar shifts from things you *have* to do to things you *want* to do.

2. *Margin.* This refers to financial margin. You aren't living paycheck to paycheck, and no one else has a claim on your money. You are free to financially support the things you're passionate about or to respond to an emergency need without worrying about putting your family in a bind. You can give generously and quickly, because you know you can afford it.

3. *Options.* By options, I mean you've got the power to make choices. You aren't weighed down by financial obligations or calendar restrictions. Instead of feeling like you're under the thumb of an employer or a mortgage lender, you're taking control of your own decisions. The only one calling the shots on your time and money is you.

4. *Availability.* If you've been chained to a desk for most of your life, this is a game changer. Financial independence gives you the freedom to be there for people you care about. If an out-of-state friend calls with bad news, you can hop on a plane immediately without asking for anyone's permission. You can respond in an instant, because you have the time and money to be there for anyone, anywhere, anytime.

This kind of freedom changes you, inside and out.

But what about those who don't become financially independent at any point in their lives? What does life look like for them? To be blunt—it often doesn't look good. Vanguard reports that the average 401(k) balance in America is $103,866.[36] That takes into account all age groups, from those under twenty-five to those over sixty-five. Obviously, younger folks are going to have less saved than their parents and grandparents, so let's just look at the over-sixty-five group. The average 401(k) balance in that group is $209,984.[37] If that represents *all* of an average person's retirement savings, then they're in trouble. Using the industry standard 4% annual withdrawal, this person is looking at an annual retirement income of—wait for it— $8,000. That's less than $700 *per month*. Can you live on that now? I can't. Will that fund your high-definition retirement dream? It won't fund mine. And yet that's how more and more families are hitting their retirement years, realizing the nest egg they *thought* would support them simply can't. And so they keep working, depend on Social Security, and pray they stay healthy.

Even if they do stay relatively healthy, though, Medicare premiums alone can wreck their finances. CNN Money reports that the typical healthy, sixty-five-year-old couple can expect to spend $266,600 on Medicare premiums alone throughout their retirement years, and that doesn't even include out-of-pocket expenses or long-term care costs.[38] So, if the average person that age has $209,984 in their 401(k) and he can expect to spend $266,600 on premiums alone for himself and his spouse, you can see the train wreck happening in slow motion. If they don't find some other source of income, they'll be moving in with their kids or falling for some trashy reverse-mortgage sales pitch. Don't let that be your plan for retirement.

I know that saving for the long term can seem overwhelming, especially with the immediate needs of the present. But the kinds of financial limitations mentioned above don't just hurt your future retirement; they hurt how well you can live your life in the here and now. Financial independence brings flexibility, margin, options, and availability—but you don't have those things when you're living a life stuck in debt and out-of-control spending. For example, many years ago our family heard about another family in our church who had lost everything in a fire. Our hearts broke for them, and we wanted to do something huge to help them. But when we really thought it through, we couldn't. We couldn't afford to help them—not as much as we wanted to, anyway. We were still in debt at the time, and we were working our tails off to clean up the mess we had made for ourselves. In choosing to obligate myself to Visa, I had chosen *not* to be available to help other people when they really needed it. It felt like I was in financial handcuffs, and it added even more fuel to my fire to get my act together. Maybe you know what that feels like. When faced with that lack of freedom, you can either give up and stay there forever or can get mad and change your situation. Too many people give up. Millionaire-minded people don't.

If you're determined to hit the millionaire mark, start thinking about what you will do with the freedom that comes with financial independence. Don't just daydream about it; write down specific things you want to do. What will it look like to have that kind of freedom, flexibility, margin, options, and availability? How will you take advantage of the time and money that will be available to you? Put that vision down on paper. Make it a goal for your family and keep that goal close.

CONSIDERATIONS FOR THE FINANCIALLY INDEPENDENT

If financial independence is the top of the mountain you're climbing, you may be tempted when you get there to reach the top and scream, "I did it! I'm a millionaire!" Go for it. You'll deserve to celebrate. It's not all sunshine and celebrations at the top, though. Lifestyle creep, starting to spend more just because you have more, has a way of sneaking in and eating away at the wealth you've built up, so you've got to stay plugged into your finances and make sure you're continually making smart choices. That comes down to two big considerations: protecting your wealth and managing the lifestyle changes a $1 million net worth may bring. I could fill another whole book with this stuff, but let's at least get a high-level view of things to consider.

Protecting Your Financial Independence

The first step in protecting your financial independence is to make sure you have a rock-solid defense. It takes an enormous amount of hard work and years of effort to become a millionaire; you don't want to lose it all overnight because you didn't take the time to properly protect it. That protection comes in the form of insurance. I know that insurance isn't the most exciting purchase you could make with all that hard-earned money, but you don't want to work thirty years for something only to have a lawsuit-happy scumbag drive off with it after a minor fender-bender. There are eight types of insurance you need to add to your financial plan. The ins and outs of insurance are more than we can get into here, but I at least want to give you a heads-up on these eight key pieces of your wealth-building puzzle:

1. Term Life Insurance
2. Car Insurance
3. Homeowners or Renter's Insurance
4. Umbrella Policy (extra liability coverage)
5. Health Insurance
6. Long-Term Disability Insurance
7. Long-Term Care Insurance (age sixty and up)
8. Identity Theft Protection

If you don't have all of these in place, I want you to call your insurance agent *today*.

Besides insurance, you also need to make sure you've got your bridge period covered. I talked about this in chapter 8. As a quick reminder, if you think you'll want to retire before age fifty-nine and a half, you need to have some money set aside separate from your 401(k), IRA, and other retirement funds. I recommend opening a regular mutual fund and contributing over and above what you're investing into retirement accounts if a bridge period applies to you. You'll lose a ton of money in taxes and penalties if you try to crack open your retirement accounts early, so don't even consider it. Instead, make sure you've got enough money set aside somewhere else to live on between the time you leave work and when you can fully access your retirement funds. This becomes a lot easier once you pay off your home, by the way. You can throw your old mortgage payment into a mutual fund every month to build up an early-retirement account. And if you max out your 401(k) and IRA contributions for the year, a simple mutual fund is a great option for extra investing. Even if you don't need it for early retirement, it'll still be there growing over time and adding to your net worth.

Last, as I've said several times, never stop budgeting. Your budget will be the grease in the gears of your wealth-building engine; it'll keep things running smoothly for the rest of your life. You will never outgrow the need for careful budgeting, so settle in and get used to it for the long haul.

Keeping Your Lifestyle in Check

When you achieve financial independence, you'll discover you have more choices in how you spend money and what kind of lifestyle you want for yourself and your family. We've seen that most millionaires are surprisingly frugal with their lifestyle expenses, but that doesn't mean you should hunker down, drive thirty-year-old beater cars, and never enjoy your money. At that point, you're a millionaire! It's okay to enjoy the fruit of all your hard work. You just need to do it with some wisdom and intentionality. For example, if you've got $3 million in the bank and you've always dreamed of buying *that* $50,000 brand-new pickup truck, go for it. It's not going to wreck your finances. Think about the cost in proportion to your wealth. A $50,000 new car can destroy you when you're flat broke, but it's barely a blip on the radar when you've got $3 million. But this only applies if you've paid off your house and have truly achieved financial independence. If you're not there yet, a brand-new car should be the last thing on your mind.

Financial independence gives you plenty of other amazing, new options when it comes to your lifestyle. Take Anna and Neal, for example. None of their family and friends—including their own children—has any idea of this Florida couples' net worth, but Anna and Neal are living their early retirement dream.

EVERYDAY MILLIONAIRES

Anna was born in Germany, but her parents immigrated to the United States when she was nine years old. The family moved in with Anna's aunt in southern Florida, and her father got a job as a property caretaker as the family got acclimated and learned to speak and read English. The immigrant family never had a lot of money, but Anna is grateful that they never lacked for the things that really mattered.

Anna began working right out of college. She also met and married Neal, who she says grew up in a "well-off" family. Well-off or not, they never received any inheritance from either family and were on their own from day one, each working two jobs in the early years of their marriage to get off to a good start. Neal spent his entire career as a computer programmer working in IT, but Anna tried her hand at several different jobs. She spent the first seventeen years of her career at an insurance company, then switched to part-time retail work when she and Neal had kids. She later did some IT work before moving on to a position in the admissions department of a law school, where she ultimately retired from. Looking back, she said she and Neal were both paid well through-out their working lives, but their salaries were "nothing extraordinary." The key to their wealth wasn't high-paying jobs; it was what they *did* with those incomes.

The couple originally set a goal to retire at age forty-five. To get there, they put as much money into their 401(k) plans and other invest-ments (for the bridge period) as possible throughout their careers. They kept their investing strategy simple and let the 401(k) do its work. Their focus was on continually increasing contributions and always taking every penny of their employer matches. They never missed any money that was automatically deducted out of their paychecks, Anna said, so staying committed to the 401(k) was easy. The couple kept their spending in check, lived in a modest house, and even shared one car for a long time. Whatever they didn't spend, they put into their investments. Eventually, all that hard work paid off. The couple missed their early retirement goal by a few years, but they both retired at age fifty with plenty of money—over $2 million in net worth—to live on for the rest of their lives.

Today, Anna and Neal are living their lifelong dream of traveling the world. Their lifestyle has changed a lot, but it's changed in ways most people wouldn't notice. They still live simple lives, but travel has become a huge part of their world. They're also enjoying the freedom that comes with financial independence. They can do whatever they want any day of the week. If they wake up on Monday and decide to head off on a spon-taneous two-week road trip, they can. They worked hard for thirty years, and now they can spend the next thirty or forty years not working at all. The best part is, nobody has a clue. Anna said, "Nobody would know that we are millionaires because we live very simply."

That's something we've seen over and over in the millionaires we studied. It turns out that, once you can afford to buy whatever you want, you may not want to anymore.

Don't Go Backward

No matter how wealthy you become, you'll always be one bad decision away from going backward. With new options come new temptations, and you'll find yourself with some unexpected and exciting opportunities to blow a hole through your investments. For example, I talked to a guy a few years ago who had just paid off his house. It was the culmination of years of hard work and sacrifice, and he was so excited he didn't know what to do with himself. You'll never guess what he did to celebrate becoming debt-free: he financed a boat. That's right, he was so proud of himself for paying off his house that he went back into debt on a stupid boat. You see, he wasn't thinking clearly. He got a quick taste of financial independence, and it made him a little crazy. He let down his guard for an hour and financial stupidity was waiting for him on the boat lot. That one dumb decision set him back years of progress. I don't want that to happen to you, so you've got to pay attention to a few traps that will stop your progress and knock you backward. These tips will help you keep your guard up.

First, and this is just a blanket rule, debt should never be an option for you. Never. For anything at any time. Once you become debt-free and accomplish the monumental goal of paying off your house, that's it. Never again, for the rest of your life, sign up for a single dollar of debt—not even for something masquerading as an *investment*. If something has debt attached, it's not an opportunity; it's an obligation—and obligations limit your freedom.

Second, watch out for *lifestyle creep*. Sure, you need to give yourself permission to spend and to have a little fun with your hard-earned money, but keep that spending in check. Remember, the wealth you build will be your sole source of income for the rest of your life. Don't be scared to have some fun with it, but make sure that nice beach house won't end up stealing years' worth of your future income. Just because you *can* buy something doesn't mean you *should*.

This is an area many millionaire couples have to work on throughout their marriage. It's easy for one spouse to get excited about the prospect of spending some money, but their partner may not be ready to flex those spending muscles yet. That makes sense. If you live a frugal life for forty years, the thought of dropping $30,000 on home renovations may scare you to death. I coached a couple through that exact situation a few years ago. The wife wanted to do a massive renovation, but her husband freaked out at the thought of dropping so much money into the project. He wasn't there yet. So, I helped them come up with a solution. I suggested they tackle the projects one room at a time. That way, they only had to spend $5,000 or so each month, and they could see instant results. That took the pressure off him, she was able to enjoy their wealth, and their home got a beautiful makeover over the course of several months. It was a win-win, but it took a little effort to get everyone on the same page. That's effort well spent, though. As we saw in the previous chapter, millionaires prioritize their marriages and relationships. Don't work together to build wealth only to let that wealth tear you apart in the end. Keep working together and enjoy the new lifestyle you chose for yourselves.

LEAVE A LEGACY

We're all chasing significance. Every day we're on the hunt for it. We're looking for the thing that gives our lives meaning and purpose. We're thinking about who we are and how we matter in the world. That chase gives us purpose; it allows us to get outside our own heads and to see beyond ourselves. When we do that, we can start to think about what kind of impact we want to have, what kind of mark we want to leave on the earth when we're gone. You see, your life matters. I don't care how wealthy or how broke you are—*you matter*. The decisions you make and the lives you touch every day change the world. It's like throwing a rock in a lake. There's an impact, and then there are ripples. You never know where those ripples will end up or who will feel them after the rock's long gone. Your wealth—and what you do with it—is just like that rock. It can make a big splash or a tiny drop in the bucket. Either way, it creates ripples in the world, and we should take just a second to consider what those ripples may look like.

Change Your Family Forever

Financial independence allows you to take care of yourself and your family in ways you've never imagined before. Think back through all the stories we've shared in this book. Can you think of a single millionaire who inherited all their wealth—or even a big piece of their wealth—from their parents? I can't, because none of them did. All the millionaires we featured in this book came from middle-class backgrounds at best and dirt-poor backgrounds at worst. The common denominator isn't how their stories started; it's how they ended. Every one of those people ended the story as millionaire, and that means they have something their parents never did: wealth that will outlive them.

We found that 92% of millionaires plan to pass their wealth to their families. Let's take a look at what that could mean for a typical millionaire family over a few generations. The implications can be mind-blowing. Let's say you started with nothing and built up a $1 million net worth before you died. You should know by now that this is completely doable for practically anyone. Imagine you have one grown child at that point, and you leave that $1 million to her as an inheritance. Of course, you would have taught her to work and build wealth herself, so she doesn't necessarily *need* that $1 million. So she sets it aside and lets it continue to grow. Thirty years later, even if your child never added a dime to that family wealth, that $1 million would have become an astounding $17.5 million financial legacy for your grandchildren. If it rolled over one more generation, continuing to grow for another thirty years, your $1 million would have grown to more than $304 million! You would have taken your family tree from dirt poor to $304 million in three generations. This is truly generational wealth. All it takes is for one person—you—to get the ball rolling. From there, momentum and compound interest take over and create an entirely new life for the people you love the most. That's an unbelievable legacy.

> **70%** of millionaires say they set some of their income aside every month to give to others.

More to Give

Your giving doesn't just have to be focused on your family, of course. There are opportunities all around to put your wealth to good use in the world. Our research found that net-worth millionaires are much more generous than the general population, as 55% of millionaires give to others regularly, compared to 28% of the general population. Some give monthly and some give as needs arise, but most—70%—say they set some of their income aside every month to give to others. Only one in ten millionaires says giving is *not* part of their personal finances. The bottom line is that millionaires are givers.

If giving in large amounts freaks you out or you don't want anyone to know you have that much money to give away, then give it anonymously. You don't need credit; the focus should be on the gift, not the giver. And if you've never practiced regular, generous giving, you have no idea what you're missing out on. No matter who you are or how much you have, giving *always* feels good. It's a fact. I've never known a millionaire to lie on his deathbed and say, "I wish I hadn't given so much to other people." Instead, they're more likely to look back on a life of giving and wish they could have done even more.

That kind of radical giving has become a huge part of many, many millionaires' lives. A great example of this is Thomas, a millionaire I told you about earlier in the book.

EVERYDAY MILLIONAIRE

As we saw in chapter 2, Thomas had a harsh life growing up. His father had a drinking problem and his mother had mental-health issues, which caused him to spend most of his youth moving around from one foster home to another. He was surrounded by poverty for most of his childhood, and that experience had a huge effect on him. Even after he moved on to college and the military, he couldn't shake the deep sadness he felt when confronted with poverty and homelessness.

After college, Thomas served four years in the Army during the Vietnam War. While he was there, his heart broke for the Vietnamese people who had nothing and practically no job prospects. After the war, he and three Army buddies started a farm co-op that now employs one hundred and twenty people. The co-op gives Vietnamese families a place to work and a steady income. Forty years later, the co-op is still running strong, and Thomas is excited to say there are third-generation co-op farmers working the fields today. He travels there twice a year and has personally donated more than $250,000 to the project, which, he says, has been one of his best investments. He loves seeing the life-change that has occurred over three generations, and he's overwhelmed that he's been able to play such a big part in so many families' lives.

Now retired with a net worth of $2.6 million, Thomas is looking back on the good work he's been able to do over the years while planning for even better work ahead. As a single guy with no kids, he's planning on spending the rest of his life giving away his wealth to causes he's passionate about. "When you help someone else," he said, "you forget about your own problems."

That kind of humble, incredibly generous spirit is contagious. That's the kind of person I want to be around. Heck, that's the kind of man or woman we should *all* want to become.

YOU'RE A MILLIONAIRE IN THE MAKING

Take a second to just imagine the freedom, flexibility, confidence, and joy you can have once you become financially independent. You'll be free to do whatever you want, whenever you want. You'll have options, flexibility, margin, and availability to spend time and money on things that matter most to you. You won't get there by accident, though. You'll only get there by following in the footsteps of the nearly eleven million millionaires in America today. As we've seen throughout this book, these men and women share a special view of the world. They defy the myths our society has perpetuated, and they model key character traits that have made them success-ful. Plus, they've lived out several key action steps I've called out throughout this book. They take ownership of their actions. They live on less than they make. They've paid off their house. They aren't scared to roll up their sleeves and work hard. They invest consistently for a long period of time in simple, commonly available retirement accounts. They practice generosity and plan to *live* a leg-acy while they're here and *leave* a legacy when they're gone. That's who they are, and that's who you need to be to join them in the ranks of America's millionaires.

I'm going to say it one last time: Anyone can become a millionaire in America today. Yes, that includes you. It's not magic. It's not luck. It's not about gender or race or region or profession. If you follow the lead of the millionaires studied in this book, and if you commit right now to do what they did, you are *already* a millionaire in the making. Whether you're a broke college student eating ramen noodles out of a Styrofoam cup or a struggling single parent working two jobs to make ends meet—*you can be a millionaire*. If you haven't already, it's time to set aside all your doubts because the possibility is available to you. The choice is yours. You have all the tools and advantages you need to get the job done. You can reach higher, dream bigger, and go further than you ever thought possible.

I've shown you what to do. And never forget: you have the power to create the financial future you want for yourself and your family. This is in your hands now. Whatever happens next—good or bad, wealthy or poor—is on you. This is your moment of decision. This is your opportunity. Make it count.

Throughout this book, I've ended every chapter with a breakdown of millionaire *dos* and *don'ts*. Here, at the end, it's time to take that a step further. Let's take everything we've learned about millionaires and turn it into a list of dos and don'ts *for you*. If you want to become a millionaire:

You Will . . .
- **Invest in "boring" company retirement plans—even if you think you can't afford it.** Remember, company-sponsored retirement plans like the 401(k) are the number one way the millionaires we studied built their wealth.
- **Build your wealth slowly and steadily over time.** 79% attribute regular, consistent investing in retirement plans over a long period of time as the reason for their success.
- **Pay off your house.** It took millionaires an average of

10.2 years to pay off their homes, and 67% of them live in homes with paid-off mortgages.

- **Live intentionally by budgeting and avoiding debt.** Remember, 93% of the millionaires we studied say they stick to the budgets they create, and 96% of millionaires never carry a balance on a credit card.
- **Go to (or send your kids to) college—probably state schools—without any student loan debt.** A total of 79% of millionaires did not attend prestigious private schools: 62% of millionaires graduated from public state schools, 8% attended community college, and 9% never graduated college at all. Also, 68% of the millionaires with a college degree never took out a penny in student loans.
- **Take responsibility for yourself.** 97% of millionaires say, "I control my own destiny."
- **Set—*and achieve*—goals for yourself.** An overwhelming majority (97%) of millionaires say they almost always achieve the goals they set for themselves.
- **Work hard. *Really* hard.** 93% of millionaires said they got there by hard work rather than big salaries.
- **Get advice from investing professionals as you go.** 68% used a financial planner to achieve their net worth.
- **Leave a financial legacy.** 92% of millionaires plan to pass their wealth to their families.
- **Practice outrageous generosity.** 70% of millionaires set some of their income aside every month to give to others.

You Won't . . .
- **Depend on a huge inheritance or a stroke of luck for your financial independence.** 79% of millionaires received zero inheritance. Only 16% of millionaires inherited more than

$100,000, and only 3% inherited $1 million or more. So, it's safe to say that at least 84% of millionaires—if not more—built their wealth on their own!

- **Need to have a high-powered, high-paying career to build wealth.** Remember, only 15% of millionaires held senior leadership positions in their careers; the rest—a whopping 85%—were regular people working regular jobs. Also, only one-third of millionaires *never* made six figures in a single working year; only 31% of them averaged $100,000 a year over the course of their career; and only 7% of them averaged $200,000 a year over the course of their career.

- **Take crazy, uncalculated risks with your money.** Not a single person in all the millionaires we interviewed mentioned single stock as a major contributor to becoming wealthy, and not one of the 10,000 millionaires we surveyed put single stock in their top three wealth-contributing factors. The number one contributing factor to millionaires' high net worth is investing in retirement plans.

- **Rely on stupid, risky, get-rich-quick schemes.** The average millionaire hit the $1 million mark for the first time at 49 years old after years—*decades*, in fact—of hard work. Only 5% of millionaires got there in ten years or less.

- **Allow your lifestyle to get out of control and eat up all your money.** Again, 94% of millionaires say they live on less than they make—compared to 55% of the general population.

- **Spend a ridiculous amount of money just to keep up with your neighbors.** Only 7% of the millionaires we studied felt pressure to keep up with their friends and families when it came to spending.

- **Quit. Ever.** Remember, 98% of millionaires—practically all of them—say they always finish what they start.

Action Steps to Become an Everyday Millionaire

A Word from Hogan

The ball is in your court, as they say.

You've learned that *anyone* can become an everyday millionaire. You've read how others made it happen.

Now it's *your* turn.

Your financial future is *your* responsibility. Nobody else can do it for you. *You* have to make the right choices. *You* have to do the work. *You* have to make the sacrifices. Oh, but the reward . . .

If you need an outline, look through the pages that follow. You'll see a clear-cut, step-by-step plan for becoming a millionaire. As you've learned, it's not rocket science. The only thing stopping you is, well, you.

But I believe in you.

It's time for you to believe in yourself.

It's time to take control of your money.

It's time to act.

I can't wait to hear your everyday millionaire story!

You CAN do this!

Chris Hogan

ACTION STEPS
to Become an Everyday Millionaire

1. Know Where You Are

2. Dream Big

3. Confirm Your Target

4. Choose Intentionality

5. Set Goals for Your Money—and Yourself

6. Partner with an Investment Professional

ACTION STEP I
Know Where You Are

You've discovered that millionaires are regular people, and you've learned that you can become one too. The first step in that process is knowing where your finances stand today. Simply put, you need to know your net worth—that's what you *own* minus what you *owe*. It's all your assets minus all your liabilities. Calculating this number is just basic math, and I've created a tool to help.

The Net Worth Calculator is simple and free to use. It takes just five minutes to complete—less time than you spend in the drive-through. We'll do the math for you. All you have to do is answer six questions about your assets and liabilities, and—just like that—you'll know exactly where you stand. We'll even give you some practical, tailored advice to set you on the path to becoming an everyday millionaire.

Get started now. Go to https://www.chrishogan360.com/networth.

It's about to get real!

ACTION STEP 2
Dream Big

Once you know your net worth, it's time to take the next step. You need to dream. What do you want your life to look like when you don't have to go to work? Do you want to travel? Start a business? Try a new hobby?

Dreaming about your future gives you a constant reference point. And it gives you an emotional boost you need to keep going when you're ready to quit!

If you're married, I want you and your spouse to set aside time to dream about your future. Get a babysitter and get away from the house. While you're on your date, I don't want you to talk about work or family or politics or the laundry. *I want you to dream together.* I want you to hear each other's hopes for the future. You don't have to pursue the *same* dreams, but you do need to support each other's dreams.

Now if you're single or newly single, I want you to dream too. Take a friend out to lunch and talk about your dreams. The point is, you have dreams to chase!

The next page has been designed been for you to write down your dreams. There are no right or wrong answers. Don't shoot down any ideas—even if you don't have the money right now. That's not the point. Your dreams give you a goal to reach.

PLACES I WANT TO GO	PEOPLE I WANT TO SEE
HOBBIES I WANT TO PURSUE	**CAUSES I WANT TO SUPPORT**
BUSINESS I WANT TO START	**WAYS I WANT TO BLESS OTHERS**

ACTION STEP 3
Confirm Your Target

If you've read this far, you probably have a good idea of the amount of wealth you want to accumulate. But in case you haven't, I have a tool to help you.

It's called the R:IQ. Provide some basic information, like your annual income, how much money you'll need each month to live out your dream, and how much you've already invested, and the tool will calculate how much you need to save every month from now until you hit your wealth target.

You can adjust the number of years you want to work, the rate of return you think you'll earn on your investments, and the withdrawal rate (the percentage of your money you'll use each month).

It's free. It's easy to use. And it gives you an HD-clear number to work toward.

Go to https://www.chrishogan360.com/riq/ and take the R:IQ. What's your number?

ACTION STEP 4
Choose Intentionality

You know your net worth. And you know how much you want to save to reach your wealth-building dreams. Now it's time to put a plan into action. Remember, millionaires are *intentional* with their money. And the best way to stay on track with your money is by keeping a budget.

If you don't have a monthly spending plan (that's all a budget is), then it's time to start one. Or, if you've gotten lazy with your finances, it's time to dust off that budget and put it back into play. Why? Because everyday millionaires create a budget—and they stick to it! I know it's not a cool or flashy concept, but it works!

Making and keeping a budget is easy with the EveryDollar tool. EveryDollar allows you to enter your take-home pay and create spending categories for your monthly expenses. And, if you're paying off debt, EveryDollar will help you stay on track with the Baby Steps that I outlined in chapter 8. There's even the option to connect your bank account to your budget so you can track your expenses as you go. No more keeping up with receipts and wondering where your money went. With EveryDollar it's all there in one place. Go to https://www.everydollar.com or download the app on your digital device to create your first budget in just ten minutes. It's that simple!

Now get to work!

ACTION STEP 5

Set Goals for Your Money—and Yourself

Once you start following a budget and you know where your money is going every month, you can set long-term goals for your money.

The goals you set will depend on where you are on the millionaire journey. Look back at the Baby Steps to determine where you are. You may need to get rid of debt. Or beef up your emergency fund. If you're debt-free, you can start setting long-term wealth-building goals.

What should those goals look like?

- **Specific**
- **Measurable**
- **Achievable**
- **Relevant**
- **Time-Sensitive**

For example, you could set the following goal:

By **December 31**, I will **save $10,000 in my emergency fund** by **taking a second job and cutting my budget by $300**.

Once you get your finances in order and set goals for your money, you'll discover the importance of setting goals for other parts of your life, too. Don't ignore these important areas:

Spiritual Growth	**Fitness**	**Education**
Family	**Relationships**	**Career**

Just use the same formula that's outlined for you above. Try setting one goal per area for now. You can add to them later!

ACTION STEP 6
Partner with an Investment Professional

You wouldn't represent yourself in court. And you wouldn't perform surgery on yourself. You'd look to professionals who have the education and experience to help you. The same principle applies to building wealth.

If you don't have an investment pro, now is the time to find one. If you don't know where to look, try our SmartVestor service. Provide your information and you will get a list of pros in your area who are ready to work with you. For more information, check out my website at https://www.chrishogan360.com/dreamteam/.

You don't have to work with the first investment professional you talk to. Interview several and choose the person who will be the right fit for your goals and needs. Here are questions to ask when you're interviewing potential investment pros:

- What kind of experience do you have?
- What certifications have you earned?
- What do you love about your job?
- What is your overall investing philosophy?
- How do you get paid?
- What financial services do you provide?
- How can I reach you to discuss questions or concerns?

Now listen up: An investment professional can provide great insight and advice, but in the end, the decision is yours.

It's your life. Take CHARGE!

Everyday Millionaires Hiding in Plain Sight

Ten years ago, my wife and I had $800,000 in debt when we finally woke up. We have worked hard to get where we are today. We both have a high school education with a little college for me and trade school for her. With hard work, we have made a great living, but getting out of debt was key.

—BILL, $1.2 MILLION NET WORTH

Hard work and sweat equity really pay off in the long run. Becoming a millionaire is doable even on a teacher's salary.

—DORENDA, $1.1 MILLION NET WORTH

Anyone can become a millionaire or have high net worth. You just need to be committed to saving and spending less than you make.

—JAMES, $1.4 MILLION NET WORTH

I have never earned more than $38,000, and we didn't inherit any money. We taught our children to be smart with money, and they all started saving for college at young ages. No one has any clue what we are worth. And we can't wait to retire in about four years with a goal of $3 million!

—JANET, $2.5 MILLION NET WORTH

It's not easy becoming a millionaire. You have to be willing to sacrifice things. If you are more worried about what other people think of you—what you drive, where you live, and what type of clothes you wear—then you will never get to where you want to be financially.
—GARY, $14.6 MILLION NET WORTH

We are often surprised by people who say that it's impossible to get ahead. I grew up in a low-income home with a single mom. My husband is first-generation American, and his parents arrived with nothing. We just believed that if we were smart, we would get ahead.
—HELEN, $1.1 MILLION NET WORTH

We started out in 1969 newly married, owning two old suitcases and a $350 VW Beetle. Now we own two homes and four cars, and we are debt-free. We pay cash for anything we wish, including cars. If we can't afford to pay for it in cash, we don't buy it.
—TOM, $1.9 MILLION NET WORTH

Growing up in a large family, there wasn't much money. I was mostly independent by the time I was fifteen. I moved out at eighteen, bought myself a beater car, and put myself through college with scholarships and working. Growing up this way was hard, but very beneficial to me.
—STEVEN, $2.2 MILLION NET WORTH

Save early and consistently. It seems like a pipe dream at the time, but compound interest is real! Just give it time.
—JOHN, $1.4 MILLION NET WORTH

Hard work is the key. If I want to do something that is not in the budget, I earn the money through a second or third job.
—GLENN, $3.5 MILLION NET WORTH

I never pay someone for labor. Instead, I turn off the TV and make it a hobby of mine to learn whatever skills are needed to perform house or vehicle maintenance, manage investments, and so on.

—PAUL, $1.2 MILLION NET WORTH

The absolute secret is to spend less than you make. Live within your means and understand wants versus needs. Be willing to miss out on short-term fulfillment. No debt allows you to live on a lot less!

—DONNA, $1.1 MILLION NET WORTH

My single mother came to this country with three kids, not knowing the language. She taught us discipline and hard work. I am what I am today because of her and my uncle.

—LOUIS, $5.5 MILLION NET WORTH

All you really have to do to become wealthy is pay attention. There was a time that we made a lot of money, but we also spent a lot of money. Now we start our budget by giving and saving, and we pay attention to where the money goes.

—DAVID, $2 MILLION NET WORTH

My parents always used cash, and that's what they taught me. I've never had a car loan, credit card debt, or student loan debt. We purchased a minivan when we had twins six years ago, and we don't plan on buying another car until our kids are in college.

—TONY, $1.3 MILLION NET WORTH

We have three children. We are teaching them that anyone—anyone—can be financially independent—a millionaire plus! It is all about controlling yourself, hating debt, and investing from the second you graduate college.

—KIM, $1 MILLION NET WORTH

I started planning and saving when I read about compound interest at age thirteen. We always lived on one income and saved or invested the other. We have both been working jobs outside the home since we were eleven years old. Our parents gave us a strong work ethic and taught us not to care about what others possess. The key to getting ahead financially is compounding, time, and consistency.

—DONALD, $9.5 MILLION NET WORTH

You make your own success with hard work and dedication to long-term savings and investments. Don't focus on what others have. You control your outcome.

—SANDRA, $1.1 MILLION NET WORTH

We lived paycheck to paycheck with little savings and a low net worth. Now, eight years later we are completely debt-free with a $1.2 million net worth, a one-plus-year emergency fund, and our kids' college fund.

—SCOTT, $1.2 MILLION NET WORTH

This is a great country that provides opportunity to individuals who are disciplined enough to work hard, save, invest, and let compound interest work.

—KENNETH, $2 MILLION NET WORTH

Research Methodology

Throughout this book, you've seen statistic after statistic and read story after story of everyday, run-of-the-mill millionaires across the United States. As we said at the start of the book, this was the largest, most comprehensive study of millionaires ever conducted. We spent seven months studying more than 10,000 millionaires to truly understand who they are, what they do, how they live, and how they achieved financial independence. And, as I've said, we focused specifically on net-worth millionaires, meaning people whose total net worth was at or above the $1 million mark. That makes our research rather unique among other wealth studies. Most research on "the wealthy" focuses on high-income earners, but we think there's a big problem with that approach. Our decades of experience have shown us that "high income" does not automatically translate to "high net worth." To be blunt, there are far too many broke, financially stressed families in the country who are earning six figures. We didn't want to hear from them. We wanted to talk to millionaires—the true standard of financial independence.

For that reason, we targeted individuals with a net worth of $1 million or more, regardless of their income. We worked with millionaires in all fifty states and in every major US city, conducting in-depth phone interviews and facilitating a series of detailed research questionnaires. We talked to millionaires in the suburbs, in rural areas, and in big cities. We talked to executives and farmers. We talked to people who were retired and those who were still working. We talked to people across a wide spectrum of professions, ethnicities, and socioeconomic backgrounds. We talked to as many millionaires as we could because, as the research shows, millionaires are everywhere. Then we took that research a step further and conducted additional surveys with the general population for comparison and brought in secondary data sources when available for additional contrast and comparison.

In this book, you learned from thousands of millionaires and you read the detailed stories of about thirty. I should note, though, that we did change the names and locations of the millionaires we specifically featured. We did that with their permission and for their privacy. Like we've said, most of these men and women don't live lavish lifestyles, and their friends and neighbors would probably be shocked to learn that they're millionaires. It was our honor to get to know these incredible people, and I pray their stories have inspired you to someday join them in the ranks of America's millionaires.

Research Details
- More than 10,000 millionaires participated in this study.
- All fifty US states and top one hundred metro areas were represented.
- We conducted dozens of in-depth interviews to get behind the numbers and truly get to know these millionaires.
- All millionaires in this study answered a 119-question research survey that explored family background, career history, purchasing habits, investing strategies, and more.
- Participants were recruited by a third-party, invitation-only research panel as well as our in-house research team.
- We conducted this study over seven months from August 2017 to March 2018.

Notes

Introduction

1. Catherine Clifford, "A Record Number of Americans Are Now Millionaires, New Study Shows," *CNBC Money*, March 24, 2017, https://www.cnbc.com/2017/03/24/a-record-number-of-americans-are-now-millionaires-new-study-shows.html.

Chapter 1

2. Clifford, "Record Number.

Chapter 2

3. *Forbes 400; The List, 2017 Ranking*, https://www.forbes.com/forbes-400/list/#version:static_header:position_sortreverse:true.
4. Augustino Fontevecchia, "There Are More Self-Made Billionaires in the Forbes 400 Than Ever Before." *Forbes*, October 3, 2014, https://www.forbes.com/sites/afontevecchia/2014/10/03/there-are-more-self-made-billionaires-in-the-forbes-400-than-ever-before/#199c4b623369.
5. Fontevecchia, "Self-Made Billionaires.
6. Edward N. Wolff and Maury Gittleman, "Inheritances and the Distribution of Wealth or Whatever Happened to the Great Inheritance Boom?" Springer Science+Business Media, November 7, 2013, http://piketty.pse.ens.fr/files/WolffGittleman2013.pdf
7. George Dvorsky, "Michael Phelps: 'Naturally' Transhuman," Institute for Ethics and Emerging Technologies, August 19, 2008, https://ieet.org/index.php/IEET2/more/dvorsky20080818.
8. Richie Allen, "Michael Phelps Workout and Diet," Muscle Prodigy, December 11, 2011, https://www.muscleprodigy.com/michael-phelps-workout-and-diet/.
9. Catherine Clifford, "Five Daily Habits Olympian Michael Phelps Swears By," *MSNBC*, February 16, 2017, https://www.cnbc.com/2017/02/16/5-habits-michael-phelps-developed-that-made-him-a-winner.html.

Chapter 3

10. Investing $700 a month from age thirty to age fifty-five at an 11% rate of return would amount to $1,066,789.

Chapter 4

11. Thomas J. Stanley, *The Millionaire Mind*. Kansas City: Andrews McMeel Publishing, 2001.

12. Katie Lobosco, "Here's How Much College Will Cost You This Year," *CNN Money*, October 26, 2016, http://money.cnn.com/2016/10/26/pf/college/college-tuition-2016-2017/index.html.

13. Lobosco, "How Much."

14. Lobosco, "How Much."

15. "A Look at the Shocking Student Loan Debt Statistics for 2017," Student Loan Hero, September 13, 2017, https://studentloanhero.com/student-loan-debt-statistics/.

16. $351 invested monthly from age twenty-two to sixty-five with a 10% rate of return.

17. Anthony P. Carnevale, Stephen J. Rose, and Ban Cheah, "The College Payoff: Education, Occupations, Lifetime Earnings," The Georgetown University Center on Education and the Workforce, https://cew.georgetown.edu/wp-content/uploads/2014/11/collegepayoff-complete.pdf.

18. Investing $437 a month from age 22 to age 65 with a 10% rate of return would equal $3.4 million.

19. Emma Bowman, "What Living on $100,000 a Year Looks Like," *NPR*, December 3, 2017, https://www.npr.org/2017/12/03/567602293/what-living-on-100-000-a-year-looks-like.

20. Bowman, "Living on $100,000."

21. Bowman, "Living on $100,000."

Chapter 6

22. Ramsey Solutions, "Stress and Anxiety Surrounding Retirement," *Retirement in America Research Study*, August 22, 2016, https://cdn.ramseysolutions.net/media/company/pr/retirement_research/retirement_stress/ramsey_solutions_research_stress_retirement.pdf.

Chapter 7

23. Kelsey Mays, "What's the Average Car Payment?" Cars.com, June 16, 2017, https://www.cars.com/articles/whats-the-average-car-payment-1420695758481/.

Chapter 8

24. Mary Morrissey, "The Power of Writing Down Your Goals and Dreams," *Huffington Post*, December 6, 2017, https://www.huffingtonpost.com/marymorrissey/the-power-of-writing-down_b_12002348.html.

25. Mark J. Perry, "Homes Today Are 1,000 Square Feet Larger Than in 1973 and Living Space Per Person Has Nearly Doubled," *AEI*, June 5, 2016, http://www.aei.org/publication/new-us-homes-today-are-1000-square-feet-larger-than-in-1973-and-living-space-per-person-has-nearly-doubled/.

26. Sean Becketti, "Why America's Homebuyers and Communities Rely on the

30-Year Fixed-Rate Mortgage," FreddieMac, April 10, 2017, www.freddiemac
.com/perspectives/sean_becketti/20170410_homebuyers_communities_fixed
_mortgage.html.

27. Becketti, "America's Homebuyers."

Chapter 9

28. Rebecca Riffkin, "So Far in 2015, More Americans Exercising Frequently,"
Gallup, July 29, 2015, http://news.gallup.com/poll/184403/far-2015-americans
-exercising-frequently.aspx.
29. "Adult Obesity Facts," Center for Disease Control and Prevention, https://www
.cdc.gov/obesity/data/adult.html.

Chapter 10

30. "Only 1 in 3 Millennials Are Investing in the Stock Market," Bankrate, July 6,
2016, https://www.bankrate.com/pdfs/pr/20160706-July-Money-Pulse.pdf
31. Ally Financial Press Room, "Sixty Percent of Americans Battle the 'Someday
Scaries,' According to New Survey from Ally Invest," Ally Financial, Oct. 16,
2017, https://media.ally.com/2017-10-16-Sixty-Percent-of-Americans-Battle
-the-Someday-Scaries-According-to-New-Survey-from-Ally-Invest.
32. "Ten Important Facts about 401(k) Plans," Investment Company Institute,
August 2017, www.ici.org/pdf/ten_facts_401k.pdf.
33. "Ten Important Facts."
34. Ally Financial, "Someday Scaries."

Chapter 11

35. Clifford, "Record Number."
36. "How America Saves 2018," Vanguard, https://pressroom.vanguard.com
/nonindexed/HAS18_062018.pdf
37. "How America Saves."
38. Katie Lobosco, "Don't freak out about health care costs in retirement," *CNN
Money*, December 30, 2015, http://money.cnn.com/2015/12/30/retirement
/retirement-health-care-costs/index.html.